"This book breaks the myth that older people do not have fulfilling and passionate sex lives. It will make great bedtime reading for anyone who feels their love life needs a little help, and encourage those who already enjoy making love, whatever their age."

Julia Cole, psychosexual therapist and writer

"A valuable contribution to our understanding of sex and relationships in older couples. Full of useful insights for couples and therapists. Excellent at debunking the myths about sex and aging."

Jane Roy, Relate

"If you're one of the millions who enjoyed Bernie's *The New Male Sexuality*, you'll love *Better Than Ever*! It's vintage Zilbergeld: honest, funny, wise, helpful, and a little bit in-your-face. Bernie interviewed sexually satisfied people to learn more about how they continue to make sex enjoyable as they get older. He has taken their wisdom, techniques, lessons, and experience, added his clinical savvy and quirky way of saying things, and created a book that will benefit practically everyone."

Dr Marty Klein, sex therapist and publisher

Better Than Ever

Time for Love and Sex

Bernie Zilbergeld PhD

with George Zilbergeld PhD

Foreword by Lonnie Barbach PhD

Crown House Publishing Limited
www.crownhouse.co.uk

First published by

Crown House Publishing Ltd
Crown Buildings, Bancyfelin,
Carmarthen, Wales, SA33 5ND, UK
www.crownhouse.co.uk

British Library Cataloguing-in-Publication Data
A catalogue entry for this book is available
from the British Library.

**International Standard Book Number
1904424368**

Printed and bound in the UK by
Cromwell Press, Trowbridge, Wiltshire

*This book is dedicated to the memory of Bernie Zilbergeld,
and his parents, Sam and Clara Zilbergeld.*

Contents

Foreword

Bernie Zilbergeld died a few weeks shy of his 63rd birthday in June of 2002. Like Richard von Kraft-Ebbing and Alfred Kinsey, Bernie Zilbergeld was one of the real pioneers in the field of human sexuality. As co-director of the Sex Therapy and Counseling Unit at the University of California Medical School in San Francisco, he became one of the country's leading experts in the area of male sexuality. During the 1970s and 1980s, as concerns moved from understanding sexual functioning to solving sexual dysfunction, Bernie wrote his groundbreaking book, *Male Sexuality* (later revised as *The New Male Sexuality*). This book is *the* classic self-help guide to understanding problems of male sexuality, including rapid ejaculation and erection problems.

Bernie was also a dear friend and my professional counterpart: female sexuality being my field of expertise. We frequently discussed theoretical issues and occasionally planned workshops or presentations together. I knew him well.

Better Than Ever represents the culmination of Bernie's professional work. It also represents a high point in Bernie's personal work. The product of a difficult upbringing, Bernie found close, loving relationships a challenge. He understood sex, but he was far less an authority on intimacy. To his credit, Bernie was aware of the deficit and set about addressing it. His research for

Better Than Ever was a vehicle for learning more about the complex subject of sexuality and intimacy from the real experts: those couples who had attained sexually satisfying and deeply loving intimate relationships.

The couples' expertise expanded Bernie's professional efforts to explain an essential topic for a much-neglected population (those over 45 years old), and it also helped him to enhance his personal understanding. During the seven years that he was interviewing couples for the book, he was applying the information gleaned to his own life. He had met Marilynne, and he was bound and determined to get this relationship right—to make a solid, safe, and loving partnership the centerpiece of his life. With the insights from his research and the commitment and cooperation of a loving partner, Bernie finally achieved his goal.

Bernie knew that it wasn't all that difficult to have good sex—especially in the initial stages of a relationship. What was difficult, he recognized, was to maintain and deepen the sexuality over time, something that could only occur when it rested on the foundation of a secure emotional partnership.

With his unique point of view and quirky sense of humor, combined with the firsthand insights of his interviewees to guide him, Bernie has created a guide for couples who wish to maintain (or rekindle) a passionate and inventive sexual relationship despite the impediments that come of having spent years or decades together— with all that that entails—and the physiological interferences of the aging process. Delightful stories and anecdotes impart a variety of tools and techniques for developing the kind of openness and safety necessary to enable a couple to adapt to the variety of changes that are likely to occur after midlife.

Bernie Zilbergeld himself suffered from some serious medical problems resulting from diabetes. Although some of these problems directly affected his sexual responsiveness, they never diminished the importance or the satisfaction he derived from his sex life. Bernie was truly one of those for whom love and sex were actually *Better Than Ever* as he grew older.

Lonnie Barbach PhD
Author of *For Each Other* and *The Erotic Edge*

Introduction

When I set out to write a book on sex and aging, I had no idea where it would lead me. I had been a sex therapist for 27 years, had attended numerous conferences, had written several books, and had worked with hundreds of midlife and older clients, and yet I didn't think I knew enough about the subject. In fact, I didn't think anybody did. We know lots about sex and adolescents because students are easy to study, but we know very little about sex among older people—so little in fact that some people mistake lack of information for lack of activity. My son Ian, 13 years old at the beginning of this project, who until that moment I thought was well educated about sex and love, told me that my book was a waste of time. "No one will want to read it," he stated adamantly. Incredulous, I asked why he thought that. His response floored me: "Because everyone knows that people over 40 don't have sex." Everyone except for his apparently demented father, I guess.

Now that I have finished the research on the book, I am happy to report that people over 40, over 50, over 60, and over 70 and 80 are not only having sex, some of them are having the best sex of their lives. That's why I call the book *Better Than Ever*. But as excited as I am about my research, I want to stress that I am not one of those people who promise baby boomers constant bliss or eternal youth. The fact is, sex changes as you age. There are certain realities that have to be confronted. You are probably going to get to know your doctor much better as you get older—and your pharmacist. This is often the time of increasing physical disabilities and illness and medical interventions. However, while you may slow down and your lovemaking may be different than it was in your youth, that doesn't mean that the quality has to be lower or your pleasure less.

Mature sex is different and it is better than ever

I always stayed in good physical condition—I did some kind of exercise almost every day and could out walk almost everyone I knew. I felt like I was 25 or 30. I somehow overlooked the fact that I had a daughter who was herself over 30 years old. I ignored the reality that I tired more easily than I used to and could no longer stay up late and be raring to go early the next day, that I usually had a number of aches in my shoulder, neck, and back when I got out of bed in the morning, and that I was developing a roll of fat around my waist, despite the hundreds of crunches I did every week and my healthy diet that included lots of fruits and veggies.

My first reality check was in 1995 at the age of 56 when I met a very attractive and sexy woman. During an early conversation, she remarked that frequent, high-quality sex was an essential ingredient of any good relationship. My initial reaction was one of delight: "Oh boy. That's suits me." But when I went home, I broke into a cold sweat. My mind jumped from the Bernie of 1995 to the Bernie of 1967.

In 1967, I was living in San Francisco and participating in what came to be called the 'Summer of Love'. Actually, it was the summer of casual sex. Rock music was pulsating indoors and out, the smell of marijuana was everywhere, and the sexual revolution was at its peak. I had my share of casual sex. And although the sex didn't feel all that great (casual sex really isn't my cup of tea), it did give me a picture of myself as a sexually confident, virile man. I could get it up and on with women I hardly knew—in fact didn't know at all. At the time, that made me feel good about myself, at least for a few months.

Fast forward to 1995. Although I had done my best to deny it, there were signs that my body wasn't what it used to be. When I say my body, I really mean my penis. It had been a good friend to me for many years, but now it was a mere shadow of its former self. Once during the 'Summer of Love' I had intercourse and orgasm seven times in eight hours; three decades later, I probably couldn't have intercourse seven times in a week. As for seven orgasms in eight hours, I won't even get into that. I finally had to face it—I could no longer count on my penis. Sometimes it would be fine, ready for action, but at other times, even though I felt excited and the conditions were perfect, it refused to be roused from its slumber.

Being a sex therapist and having more knowledge about sexual functioning than most people, I knew what was going on. The diabetes I had since the age of 20 was starting to take its toll. Undoubtedly, I was undergoing nerve degeneration (diabetic neuropathy), which in turn was causing the unreliable erections. It was a chilling experience to confront my declining sexual abilities. Further, I was worried that I might not be sexually adequate for the new woman in my life.

Ultimately, the effects of aging on sexuality did not prevent me from having a relationship with this wonderful woman. What's more, I soon realized that she hadn't escaped the aging process either. Vaginal lubrication was a definite problem for her, and neither daily exercise nor her careful diet allowed her to shed the 15 pounds she had recently gained. These were not major issues since we used artificial lubricants happily and I loved her body as it was, but they did serve as additional reminders that things were not the way they used to be.

For me, things changed even more dramatically in the following years when I was forced to take an 18-month sabbatical from writing this book to take care of my worsening diabetes-related health problems. My penis stopped working completely, and no amount of Viagra could help. I also developed a life-threatening inability to process food. At the same time, I began a fulfilling new relationship, now three years old, and it is the best of my life—in and out of bed. Marilynne and I have a very good sex life despite the fact that my sexual abilities have been shot to hell.

I cannot match the Bernie of 1967 physically, but I am a better lover than I was 30 years ago and certainly better than I was when I first started having sex at age 19. I would not have gone to bed with me back then. I was so self-centered, I hardly noticed who I was with. But like a fine wine, I have gotten better as I have aged. I now know how to give and how to receive pleasure—emotional as well as physical—in ways that I couldn't when I was younger. I am much more satisfied, and according to my partner, I can satisfy her again and again. My penis doesn't work, but my tongue works very well; I have sensitive hands, and I am a good kisser. Like many people in my research sample I can say—at the age of 62—that sex is *Better Than Ever*.

The Lovers

For this book, I conducted 145 interviews with men and women aged 45 to 87. A good number of those I interviewed are, like me, having great sex, some in long-established relationships, some in new relationships. I call these people the 'Lovers'. These Lovers are masters in the area of sexuality. (I would rather listen to them on the topic of sex than to most therapists, unless of course, the therapists are also Lovers.) If I wanted to learn to play golf, I would try to get Tiger Woods as a teacher. I'm not going to request instruction from someone who plays a mediocre game once a week. I want Tiger. If I can't get him for a teacher, at least I can go and watch him and learn from him. If I want to have a good sex life, I want to learn from the Lovers who have fabulous sex lives and are willing to share their stories.

Better than ever

The vast majority of the Lovers say that the quality of the sex they're having now is as good as or better than the sex they had when they were younger. The orgasmic rate among the Lovers is extremely high for both women and men. In fact, it is higher than most surveys have found for young women aged 18–25. So a woman in her 70s who is having a good, active sex life is probably much more orgasmic than the average 23-year-old woman.

You can have good sex even when you have serious medical problems

Before I started my research, most of what I'd read about mature sex maintained that older people can have rich sex lives only as long as they stay healthy. That turns out not to be true. Some of the Lovers are having high-quality sex in the face of medical conditions as bad or worse than mine, including heart disease, cancer, and lots of medication with a variety of side effects. The fact is that most people do not trot along in great shape and then suddenly keel over dead. People get sick. They have chronic illnesses—and they continue to have sex. And if they are Lovers, they have exceptionally good sex.

Of course, all of us want the best health and vitality for our partners and ourselves. But it is crucial to recognize that the importance of good health to satisfying sexuality in later life has been grossly exaggerated. Loving expression is possible almost regardless of what kind of physical condition you are in. I devote a whole chapter to this topic.

There are things to be learned

Throughout human history, we have engaged in a search for wondrous things—for example, ways to stave off death or, failing that, finding the fountain of youth. A look at any of the women's magazines shows that search continues. We are constantly told that while we might be getting older, we don't have to look it or feel it.

On another front, finding the secrets to happy relationships and sizzling sexuality receive tremendous attention. Bookstore shelves are filled with publications purporting to give us the keys to both.

But in this book we will be more realistic. In the last ten years, for example, we have learned how good relationships differ from mediocre and disappointing ones. Thanks to the research of John Gottman of the University of Washington in Seattle, and the writings of Lonnie Barbach and David Geisinger, it is now possible to learn and to implement the behaviors of happy couples.

I believe that with my own research, the basis for this book, I have made a modest contribution toward understanding what it takes to have exciting sex over time. The Lovers I studied had a lot in common with each other and differed in many ways from those with less interesting sex lives. Their commonalities are the 'secrets' of good loving. I have identified and examined these behaviors and presented them in Part 2 of the book. It's as if the Lovers have taken a course the rest of us missed. They seem to know things the rest of us don't.

The happy news is that these 'secrets' are not numerous or arcane. Anybody who is interested can learn them. How do I know this? Simple. When I offer their knowledge and skills to others—clients and friends—and these lessons are taken to heart, these people become more like the Lovers, much more satisfied with their sex lives.

It is never too late

There are many paths to becoming a Lover, but whichever one you choose, remember, it is never too late to *choose*. The possibility of a sexual second chance is always there. Some of the Lovers have always had it together sexually, but others have had their share of bad relationships, bad sex, and divorces. At some point, though, they decided to change. They became more open, more flexible and more willing to acknowledge the role they played in their unsatisfying sexual relationships instead of blaming it all on somebody else. They were then able, either with the same or a new partner, to create a more fulfilling sex life. So, no matter your history, if you are willing to make changes, it is never too late. Good relationships and good sex are available.

Of course, not all of the people I interviewed were Lovers. A number of them, the Non-lovers if you will, are having no partner sex or are having less-than-satisfactory sex. These people are instructive too because their self-confessed weaknesses highlight the Lovers' strengths. Where the Lovers accept their partners as they are, the non-Lovers complain, judge, and try to change their partners. Where the Lovers talk about sex, the non-Lovers stay silent. Whereas Lovers are open to reality and change, the Non-lovers are closed and insist that things have to be just so. The result is ordinary or disappointing sex rather than extraordinary sex, or no sex at all.

Who is this book for?

I believe this book is useful for anyone who wants to learn about the actual and potential sexuality of women and men no longer young: adults at midlife or beyond who want to enhance their own lovemaking. I also assume that professional helpers who work with the intimate aspects of the lives of mature adults—nurses, physicians, psychologists, marriage counselors, and social workers—will take an interest.

I also sincerely believe that young folks, even those in their 20s, can benefit from a careful reading of my words—and those of their elders. For almost two years I have been loaning early drafts of my chapters to clients over the age of 40 or so, and the vast majority said they benefited from their reading. Then I decided to run an experiment and started doing the same thing with younger clients, some in their 20s. I thought that at least some of the youngsters would gain something provided they could get beyond the 'us versus the old geezer' dichotomy. I was happily surprised when it turned out that the vast majority of the younger clients also reported learning something from their reading. Lovemaking is lovemaking. Age has less to do with it than you may think. One additional benefit for the younger crowd: a number of them said reading the material made them feel much better about what they had to look forward to. Some said it was exhilarating to read that great sex was possible in the decades ahead.

Organization

I have divided the book into two parts. In Part 1, I look at the myths about sex and aging that abound in our society. I discuss normal age-related changes, both physical and emotional. I consider obstacles to good sex as one gets older, including disease and other physical issues such as the effects of medicine and various medical interventions, as well as relationship problems. At the end of the first part, I look at sex at different times of life and detail the advantages of sex when one is older.

In Part 2, Lovers and the Non-lovers are profiled and I analyze their differing behaviors and attitudes. Here is where we look at the 'secrets' of the Lovers, where we learn exactly what they do to create and maintain their eroticism. While some of what they do makes immediate sense and evokes a gut reaction "of course", other behaviors will be surprising, at least to some readers. I know I had this reaction to a number of the findings. We don't know as much about sexuality, especially good sex, as we may think.

Research methods

I should say a few things about my research methods and my research sample. My sample was one of convenience. I started with people I knew and went from there. I was not looking for good sex or bad sex, just for people over 45. People I interviewed often spread the word, and then friends of friends, and in some cases relatives, would volunteer to be interviewed. I also ran an ad in a now-defunct newsletter, *Men's Confidential*, asking for people who would be willing to talk about their sex lives. In order to attract still more volunteers, I also pitched my research in several public talks. Toward the end of my research, I was looking for a larger sample of Lovers, so I asked only for those people over 45 who were happy with their sex lives.

To encourage people to open up about the sensitive topic of sex, I guaranteed anonymity. Many people took this promise seriously. Many contacted me by voice-mail, and I never had a clue as to their real names or whereabouts. Once we agreed on a day and time for the interview, they gave me a phone number to call. I couldn't reveal who they were even if I wanted to. A number of people asked that I not tape record the interview but just take notes. Several who agreed to the taping requested that I do the transcription rather than turn it over to someone else to transcribe. This was real torture, but it was worth it because I got invaluable information from almost every one of my interviewees. In order to carry out the promise of anonymity, I have not used real names and have taken the liberty of changing identifying information.

As far as I can tell, my sample is composed primarily of people who are middle or upper class, heterosexual, and American-born. Only a few had accents, suggesting that they may have been brought up elsewhere. I tried to increase my sample of homosexuals and lesbians but got only a few of each. Because of the small number, I cannot make any generalizations based on sexual orientation. I treat the homosexuals and lesbians in my sample as additional voices on the topic. I checked out many of the area codes given to me via email and was happy to see that they covered the entire United States.

While my sample is quite diverse, I cannot say that my findings are true of the American population in general. My findings are limited to the people I interviewed and to people like them. Nonetheless, I have reason to believe that the conclusions are widely applicable. When I use the lessons learned from the Lovers with my clients, people with troubled sex lives, they tend to improve.

How do I know my interviewees were truthful in what they told me? To be honest, I don't. Validity is a problem in all research based on self-reports, especially on sensitive topics such as income, love, and sex. In July of 2000, *The New York Times* published an article called: "Truth or Lies? In Sex Surveys, You Never Know." However, there are several reasons to believe that the respondents were being honest. One I have already mentioned: the concern a number of them expressed about confidentiality. If you're going to make up stories, why worry about anonymity? The fact that so many did care at least suggests they planned to be truthful.

In a number of cases, I interviewed both partners in a relationship separately. I was amazed by how closely their accounts matched. To be sure, there were minor discrepancies regarding dates and other things. In most respects, however, their reports were similar, especially on their global ratings about the quality of the relationship and of their sex life. In some cases, one partner would give, say, a rating of "excellent" and the other would give it a "very good", the next highest response. (In only one case did a couple differ significantly in the rating of the quality of sex. I did not use their material.) Since I doubt my interviews were important enough for a couple to get together and concoct a story, this suggests they were each giving a truthful account. The last reason to assume honesty is that there really isn't much reason to lie, especially for women. While it is known that men often exaggerate their sexual exploits, why would a 70-year-old woman overstate the number of partners she's had or the quality of her sex life? In those cases where I interviewed both partners, there was no evidence of the men exaggerating or embellishing. What the man said was corroborated by what his partner said, and vice versa. In summary, I believe there is enough evidence to suggest that the interviews yielded the truthful experiences and perspectives.

All told, I interviewed 145 men and women, 80 of whom reported gratifying sex lives. Some readers may wonder if that's a large enough sample on which to make generalizations. My answer goes like this. Although one can always complain the sample is too small, limitations of time, money, and other resources dictate that every survey end at some point. I could have done more interviews, but it seemed pointless. After about 50 of them, the interview answers became redundant. This was true for both the Lovers and the others. And although each new interview introduced some novel details, the main points and conclusions remained the same.

In fact, some months after I completed the research, I became anxious. Maybe I hadn't done enough interviews. Maybe there were important facts I had simply missed because I hadn't talked to enough people. What a fool I'd look like in the media and at professional meetings. People would point their fingers at me, and belittle my findings: "He didn't even know X", X standing for some incredibly important and yet obvious fact. In the midst of this crisis, I met a couple. Marilynne and I immediately recognized them as fellow Lovers. It didn't take me long to ask if they would consent to an interview. What a sense of relief I felt after I transcribed the interview tapes and realized that despite being a very happy, accomplished, and sexually healthy couple, they had essentially taught me nothing new. Several months later, almost exactly the same thing happened again with yet another couple. I am now quite comfortable that my sample was more than adequate.

I want to say something about topics I do not cover in this book. Although AIDS and other sexually transmitted diseases affect mature women and men as well as younger ones, I decided not to address this subject here. There is a wealth of resources for anyone who wants to learn about them and there seemed little point in addressing issues that are covered more comprehensively elsewhere.

Although I mention masturbation here and there, I do not give it much space. I realize, of course, that masturbation can be useful for learning about one's own responses and for starting to deal with some sexual problems. (I have written in detail about this aspect of masturbation in *The New Male Sexuality*, and Lonnie Barbach has written about it from a female perspective in *For Yourself* and *For Each Other*.) Masturbation is useful for providing relief when one does not have a partner, and it is also generally the quickest route to orgasm. But that's not what is important about sex to me. It's the connection and the relating that I enjoy most of all, and that is what I have chosen to write about.

A few words on language

Not until I started letting colleagues and my editor see drafts of some of the chapters did realize what a problem I faced regarding the language I was using. Most of the trouble had to do with what to call the people I was talking about, those over 45 years old. Several people objected to the term 'senior' and 'senior citizen' although neither option bothered me. 'Oldster' and 'elder' irritated others. My son Ian, who, as you've already learned, is my most blunt sounding board, first came up with 'old fart', which he then insisted was just a joke. After he stopped giggling, the best he could do was 'old people', which I didn't care for. After spending far more time than anticipated rummaging through dictionaries and thesauri, and talking to all sorts of women and men about the issue, I understood that there is no acceptable term for this group of people. I often just call them 'mature(s)'. Some thought this sounded silly, but at least no one had strong objections. Occasionally I do use senior or elder because I'm tired of writing mature. I truly wish there was a widely accepted term. Since there isn't, I'm doing the best I can and I hope the reader will give me some latitude.

When it comes to one's partner, I use a variety of terms: 'spouse' (even though not all of my couples are married), 'mate', 'sweetheart', and 'partner'. I try to reserve the term 'lover' for those who are having great sex, where I always use a capital L.

While on the subject of what to call things, I want to explain why I include myself in the baby boomers category, a frequently used term in the book, when I am seven years too old for the formal definition. Despite this fact, I have identified with the baby boomers since my graduate school days, the days of the 'Summer of Love', the counterculture, the anti-war demonstrations, and the civil rights movement. I took part in all these activities and was an especially strong and active participant in the cult of sex, drugs, and rock'n'roll. I'm not trying to fool anyone, my age is no secret, but this is the generation I have identified with my whole adult life.

Enough introduction for now. It's time to move on to what I believe is an amazing story, an account of how one of the most widely and deeply held cultural beliefs of our time has turned out to be blatantly false and of no value to anyone. It's time to look with open eyes and open minds at the true relationship between aging and sexuality, and to determine, for each individual and each couple, how we can use this information to enhance the quality of our own love lives.

Part 1

Chapter 1

Myths and Realities About Sex and Aging

Q: How many 50-year-olds does it take to screw in a light bulb?
A: None. Their screwing days are over.

American society does not have anything like the Chinese, Japanese, Indian, and Native American traditions of respecting and venerating the older generation. Elders are nothing special to us, at least not in a positive sense. This country was founded and settled by young rebels and misfits, and most immigrants have also been young. In the first census done in this country, in 1790, half the population was under 16 years old!

There is ample evidence of our largely negative view of the aged. Old people are generally thought of as pathetic, cranky, slow, inflexible, selfish, interested only in their own travails, especially their physical ailments, and a huge drain on society. Think of it; one of the most common qualifiers when talking about older people is 'fart', as in 'old fart'. Can you think of any other age group (or ethnic or religious group, for that matter), labeled in such a way? I don't think so. Although it is no longer acceptable to use derogatory terms such as 'nigger', 'kike', 'wop', or 'spic' in public, and doing so has cost people their jobs and reputations, we think nothing of saying 'old fart', 'old biddie', 'old kvetch' (for those unfamiliar with it, 'kvetch' is a Yiddish term meaning 'complaint'), 'hag', 'old lecher', and so on. If it refers to someone of a different race or ethnic background, better watch your step. But if it refers to seniors, you can say whatever you please.

In the early days of his long career researching aging, Ken Dychtwald, author of *Age Wave* and *Age Power*, said:

> I began to see that we had designed our modern world, top to bottom, to match the size, shape, and style of youth from the height of the steps in our public buildings to the length of time it takes for traffic lights to change, from the size of the typeface in our newspapers and magazines to the auditory range in our telephones and televisions, from the age and style of the models in advertisements to our embarrassment about our birthdays. In thousands of ways, over and over, we were being influenced to like what's young and dislike what's old (1999, p. xvi).

As far as America goes, people over 50 hardly exist. Not only don't we see them in the media as being thoughtful, productive, active, and all the good things, we barely see them at all. Opportunities for actors, especially women, diminish dramatically with age. An article in *The New York Times* on the topic quotes Peter Mark Richman, chairman of the Screen Actors Guild's seniors committee. He notes that 65 percent of the jobs on prime-time television go to actors aged 25 to 40 and only 6 percent to those over 60, despite the fact that Americans over 50 represent a full quarter of America's population (Whitaker, 2002, p. 8).

There's no doubt that we as a society hold views about sex and mature people that can only be called fantastic, and that's being generous. As I pointed out in the Introduction, even my sexually well-educated son believed them.

Since mistaken beliefs cause lots of damage and because there is evidence they can be changed, I think it's worthwhile discussing in more detail the pervasiveness of the main myths about sex and aging in our society and contrasting them with some of the realities.

Myths

'Myth', as I use the term, means a belief that, while it may be based on a kernel of truth, it is largely or completely untrue. We have myths in all aspects of life, especially in sensitive areas such as aging and sexuality because it's more convenient and easier to accept a myth, just like a stereotype, than discover the truth. These myths are reinforced by the whole apparatus of society. They are the messages you hear in jokes, view in movies and videos, and read in fiction. They can even be found in books and articles that purport to be nonfictional. Because 'entertainment' isn't taken seriously, we don't expect to learn anything, and so we rarely scrutinize the messages it carries, thus making it easy for all sorts of negative messages to get through to us without our being aware of them. Pretty soon we start thinking of these messages as reality, instead of what they actually are—biased points of view, and sales pitches. My main reference points for discussing the following four myths about sex and aging are common jokes, stories, and movies, because these are some of the main ways we convey and reinforce cultural beliefs.

Myth #1: mature sex doesn't exist

Think about it. When was the last time you read a novel, heard a joke, saw a TV show, video, or movie that depicted or even mentioned a sexual relationship between matures? Jack Nicholson and Diane Keaton created quite a stir in *Something's Gotta Give* because of the clear message that they were both still sexually active and interested. What the media emphasize, over and over, is sex among the young, the beautiful, and the newly acquainted and that older male Hollywood stars like Sean Connery, Clint Eastwood, Harrison Ford, Al Pacino, or Robert Redford usually end up being sexual with women half or quarter their ages.

So the main overriding myth about mature sex is that it doesn't exist. After a certain age, people just don't have sex. Or maybe they do, but only on special occasions such as wedding anniversaries or the spring solstice. Comedians like Jay Leno regularly denigrate the elderly, making jokes at their expense about adult diapers, memory lapses, nonexistent sex, and so forth.

Even some of our leading researchers have contributed to the idea that sex isn't for seniors. Kinsey and Masters & Johnson, for example, deserve some credit for talking about sex among matures. Yet when you look at their research, it's clear that the number of people over fifty studied was minuscule. It's easy to conclude from their absence, that most older people just don't have sex. An even graver error was made recently when several researchers conducted what is widely considered the best sex survey ever done, Sex in America (1994). Among the several thousand respondents, there was not one over 59 years old. This cut-off point was established, we are told, because resources were insufficient to include everyone. But if some ages had to be excluded, why not the 18 to 24 year olds, about which more is known, sexually and otherwise, than any other group in the country? Why not include those over 59, those about whom very little is known? This survey received an avalanche of publicity, including the cover story in *Time* magazine. Millions of people were exposed to it, and it would have been easy for them to conclude that since the over-59 crowd was not covered, there was nothing of interest to study in that group.

Myth #2: matures have no sexual interest

Not only do people believe that there is no sex in later years, they also believe that their elders like it that way because their sex drives mysteriously vanish as they age. Because there isn't a model of sex other than that based on the young, we are not used to thinking of our parents having sex, or of that nice old guy down the street or the grandmother next door. Of course, believing that older folks have no sexual interest puts us in a bind as we grow older and continue to feel desire.

Since we rarely see movies or read books where older people express erotic desire, we believe sex is for the young. Simply because we are not exposed to other views, we accept that matures and sex don't go together. One idea might be that they don't have sex simply because they lose their desire. After all, to the young, aging seems to have a lot to do with loss. One joke puts the loss of sexual interest in the context of other losses: "Being old means losing things: your glasses, keys, hair, sense of humor, and libido."

To be fair, it should be acknowledged that there are a number of losses associated with aging; we'll get to some of them in the next chapter. However, there's little correlation between a loss of childhood eyesight as one ages and a loss of desire for sex. Just because someone's memory is no longer what it once was does not necessarily mean he or she no longer remembers or cares about sex. Just because someone's sexual interest is piqued less frequently or less intensely than in youth does not mean that all interest is lost.

Myth #3: matures are sexually unattractive

Older men and women lose the appearance normally associated with sexual attractiveness as defined by our culture. The unlined and unmarked skin, the firm bodies, the graceful moves—all of this is gone. Who wants to have sex with someone with wrinkled skin, so-called liver spots on their hands, grey hair or baldness, paunches, droopy breasts, varicose and spider veins, and so forth? Certainly not anyone in their right mind! Here's how one little joke sees the relationship between aging and physique: "You're still in shape, but the shape is that of a sack of potatoes." Here's another that covers, shall we say, both ends of the spectrum: "You know you're old when your paunch enters a room ten seconds before the rest of you and when your bum exits the room ten seconds after the front of you."

We are inundated by ads telling us what we must do to look more youthful. If we can't be young, at least we can look the part. Magical creams prevent or dissolve wrinkles or get rid of the dreaded cellulite; this or that diet or exercise regimen dissolves fat around the middle, replacing it with flat or six-pack abdominals; this gizmo perks up your breasts; this concoction prevents or destroys liver spots; and on and on. No matter the cost or inconvenience, we'll do almost anything to look youthful, to make us more attractive to real, potential, or imagined partners, make us feel better, perhaps even make us more productive and useful. The message is quite powerful: young is beautiful and desirable; old is ugly and undesirable. And matures themselves often accept the judgements of others. Comedian Milton Berle made fun of his diminished sexual attractiveness: "At my age, when a girl flirts with me in the movies, she's after my popcorn."

And what do you make of the following from three popular novels. In the first, Clive Cussler has this passage about his hero's perception of his soon-to-be lady love: "The sunlight came through the windows of the lounge and shone on her hair, which was loose and flowing about her shoulders, and he caught the scent of her perfume. ... She was not young but a confident woman in the prime of her early thirties..." Early thirties is not young! Come on, Clive, give us a break. What exactly do you consider young? Twenty? Fifteen? Six? Still in the womb?

Another best-selling author, David Baldacci, describes a female character this way: "Gwen had aged very well. She was, he figured, in her mid- to late-thirties. Her blond hair was still long. Her figure was that of a woman ten years younger, with curves where men enjoyed seeing them and a bosom that would never fail to draw stares." (Baldacci, 2001, p. 262). Why ten years younger? Is it so surprising that there are very sexy, good-looking women with great curves and bosoms in their thirties, forties, fifties?

Finally, here's how the latest James Bond thriller describes one of the protagonists: "At fifty-two, he was still considered good-looking. Women still came on to him." (Raymond Benson, *Never Dream of Dying*, Putnam, 2001, p. 21) Why shouldn't he still be attractive at fifty-two? Where do these writers get such ideas? That's easy: they are just part of our cultural mythology, reflected and perpetuated by other authors, photographers, researchers, comedians, filmmakers, and so on.

Myth #4: matures aren't physically or sexually functional

Even if elders dug up some libido somewhere, and even if they could locate a suitable partner who didn't faint at the sight of their naked bodies, they still wouldn't have sex because their bodies don't work right. Or at least this is what the mythology tells us. Oh sure, they could hold hands, hug, or smooch a little, but this isn't sex. When it comes to the real thing, seniors just don't have what it takes. They are all used up.

Realities

The widespread belief that elders have no desire, no ability, and no activity when it comes to sex has absolutely no evidence to support it, not one shred. Every survey ever done has demonstrated that people in their 50s, 60s, 70s, and older do have desire for sex and act on that desire when they can. Although there aren't half as many surveys and studies of matures and sexuality as I would like, there are some and they tend to agree on the major findings.

A few studies on sexual interest, activity, and functioning—beginning with Alfred Kinsey in the 1940s—have focused on or at least included some mature men and women. I think it's useful to view these studies in two categories: those whose subjects were born before World

War II; and those whose subjects include the baby boomers. Let's look at two of the surveys done with respondents born long before the Second World War.

The little-known "Starr-Weiner Report on Sex and Sexuality in the Mature Years", published in 1981 (Starr & Weiner, 1981) presented the results of a study of over 800 men and women aged 60 to 91. In response to the question, "Do you like sex?" 97 percent of the respondents answered "Yes." (p. 36) That's an amazing result. In statistical studies, it's rare to see numbers over 95 percent no matter what the question. It's doubtful, for example, that we'd get 97 percent or higher if we asked, "Do you like living?" The average frequency of intercourse was 1.4 times per week and, get this, 75 percent of our respondents said that sex is the same or better than when they were younger. Quite remarkably, 36 percent of the same say that sex is better (41 percent of the females and 27 percent of the males) (p. 41). In addition, 92 percent of the sexually active women reported that their orgasm is "very important" or "somewhat important", and 86 percent said that their frequency of orgasm is the same or better than when they were younger (p. 81).

A fascinating study by Judy Bretschneider and Norma McCoy (1988) at San Francisco State University used questionnaires to measure the sexual interest and activity of 200 healthy men and women aged 80 to 102 living in retirement homes. Forty-seven percent of the men and 75 percent of the women had no regular sex partners. Seventy percent of the men and 50 percent of the women reported that they "very often" or "often" fantasized about being close and intimate with the opposite sex. The most common sexual activities engaged in were touching and caressing without sexual intercourse (82 percent of the men and 64 percent of the women reported they presently engaged in these activities at least sometimes). Next in frequency was masturbation, followed by sexual intercourse (63 percent of the men, 30 percent of the women). To give some perspective to these figures, you need to realize that the youngest respondents were born in 1900 and the older ones from 1880 to 1890, hardly a period of sexual liberalism. So much for the ideas that mature women and men aren't interested in and don't have sex.

Now consider two surveys that included at least some baby boomers—those who did grow up in a time of sexual liberation. The aforementioned "Sex in America" is a report of what is considered by sexologists, me included, to be the best survey ever done, largely because its respondents were representative of the whole American population, with one exception: the eldest subjects were only 59. Forty-nine percent of the women aged 50 to 59 and 66 percent of the men in that age range reported having sex with a partner at least a few times a month (Michael *et al*, 1994, p. 116). At all ages, those who were married or living with a partner had the most sex. What about orgasm? Over 90 percent of men in every age category reported orgasm "always" or "usually" in sex with their mates. 73 percent of women aged 50 to 59 reported orgasm "always" or "usually" in partner sex. This statistic is similar to every other age category except women aged 40 to 49 in which the corresponding percentage is 78 percent. The women with the lowest frequency of orgasm in partner sex were not the oldest ones but rather the youngest ones, aged 18 to 24. They experienced orgasm "usually" or "always" only 61 percent of the time (p. 128).

Speaking of orgasm, similar results were found in another survey where 95 percent of the men and 65 percent of the women aged 51 to 64 say they always or often have orgasm during lovemaking. This compares well to every other age group, except, as with the previous study, only 57 percent of the women in the 18-to-26-year-old group report always or often having orgasm (Janus & Janus, 1993, p. 27).

From the survey data available to us, it seems that the group most deserving of concern and support is not the over-50 crowd but rather women aged 18 to 24, insofar as frequency of orgasm. Apparently, being young and nubile has little to do with sexual satisfaction.

A more recent survey was published in 1999 by Modern Maturity, part of AARP. With over 1,300 respondents aged 45 and up, this study found that while frequency of sex diminishes with age, more than 79 percent of men and women with regular partners have intercourse at least once or twice a month. Two-thirds of the men and 61 percent of the women rated their sexual relationships as "extremely" or "very" satisfying (Modern Maturity, p. 44).

My own interviews corroborate the findings of these investigations. The vast majority of my respondents (recall they ranged in age from 45 to 89) were interested in, and having, sex although a number acknowledged it was not as special or terrific as they wished and wanted. But this had little or nothing to do with age. There are men and women at every age level whose erotic lives aren't as good as they would like.

Listen to the words of a 60-year-old Lover:

> I had a personal epiphany some months ago after seeing a movie I no longer recall. I was with my long-time friend James and he asked which women in the public eye I found most sexy. I had never considered this before and surprised myself when I blurted out 'Cokie Roberts', but when I thought about it, I realized it was true. I'd rather spend some erotic time with her than any of the young models and actresses I was familiar with. James didn't quite believe my answer, so he asked who else. Again, I surprised myself by saying Jane Seymour and Raquel Welsh as they were in the present, not how they were years ago. I realized that I find middle-aged women very sexy, far more so than the young women we're supposed to desire. The young ones are, well, just too young. Their bodies are terrific, but for me more to look at than do anything with. For arousal and activity, I'd much prefer a woman in her forties or fifties, just like my wife, who I still find an incredible turn-on after twenty-seven years.

The previously mentioned studies were done over a 60-year period and included different age groups and different research methods. Although each study can be criticized for this or that shortcoming, the results are remarkably consistent. Yes, there is a decline in sexual desire and sexual activity (masturbation, oral sex, intercourse) over the years. But before you make too much of this, it turns out that the largest decline in sexual activity takes place after a year of marriage, regardless of age (Tavris & Sadd, 1976; Rubin, L.B., 1990). Despite the decreases in desire and sexual activity, most men and women want sex, and have it if possible, into their 70s, 80s, and beyond. Not only are mature people wanting and having sex, but their enjoyment and satisfaction with it remains fairly constant over the years. The two best predictors of sexual activity in later years are (1) sexual activity in the earlier years, and (2) the availability of a sex partner. It's difficult to have sex with a partner if you don't have a partner, and this is a problem especially for women after the age of 50.

In light of this evidence—and there are more studies that could have been mentioned—how can anyone in their right mind assert that mature men and women have no interest in sex and have little or no sexual activity? The answer is simple. It can't be done, at least not if one cares about facts and accuracy.

I expect that the amount of sexual activity among those at midlife and older will increase as more and more baby boomers reach there. After all, they are the people who created, participated in, and were heavily influenced by the sexual revolution. They believe that good sex is their birthright and really don't care what anyone else thinks about it. I like the way this idea was put by a Lover aged 64:

" In the last five years I've been chided by almost everyone I know—my grown children, both of my sisters, several co-workers and, do you believe this? my priest—for my affectionate ways in public with my wife. I'm proud, I told them all, and I pity them if they're not having good loving as part of their lives. I'm a physical person and a sexual person, and I don't fancy hiding that. The day I no longer want to touch Lucy, kiss her, or make love to her is the day my life is officially over. Why should I be ashamed just because we're surrounded by a bunch of dried-up prudes? "

Sexuality is with us from the moment of birth to the moment of death. We can deny or deflect it, we can pretend it's something other than what it is, we can refuse to talk about it or act on it, we can do all sorts of things regarding our sexuality. The only thing we can't do is get rid of it.

Chapter 2

Normal Physical Changes in Men and Women at Midlife

"Aging is like cheap underwear. It creeps up on you."
—Anon.

"Old age is no place for sissies."

—Bette Davis

I know a woman who was so freaked out about her impending 50th birthday that she started torturing herself about it the day after she turned 49. You couldn't have a normal conversation with her. If somebody mentioned a number anywhere near 50 or someone else's birthday her face would fall. Her friends were too afraid to have a surprise party for her, so they tried to arrange a small dinner party, but she didn't want to hear about it. As she put it, "What's to celebrate? My life is over." She went into seclusion a few weeks before the dreaded day. Nobody knows where she went or what she did. When she resurfaced, no one was allowed to mention her birthday or her age.

While this woman is a dramatic example of someone who makes herself miserable, she is not alone in her feelings. I have seen her basic story repeated by many people. It is the zero birthdays that are especially troubling, especially for women. Twenty is okay because it means you're grown up, but for a lot of women 30 is just barely tolerable, and 40, 50 and 60 can be traumatic. For a man, the realization that he is aging tends not to happen on birthdays, but at other, less predictable times. Some event comes up and he needs a tuxedo. He goes up to the attic and finds that the tuxedo he got married in is 10 sizes too small for him. Or he joins a softball team at 40 or 50 and finds he's not as fast or agile as he used to be. Or he realizes that he's never going to be CEO or district manager. He's going to stay exactly where he is until they give him a gold watch and show him the door.

Some of these fears are based on unfulfilled expectations, but most are based on the fear of physical decline. So why not learn about the changes in body function and appearance that come with age so that we don't freak out when they happen. The changes happen at different ages for different people, but sooner or later, if you live long enough, they are going to happen to you. Read on so you won't be surprised, so you will have a heads up on the road in front of you, and the opportunity to accept the changes gracefully.

The aging body

All of us, women and men alike, hit our physical peak while in our adolescence and early twenties. After that, our bodies begin a gradual decline. While it's true that George Blanda was still kicking field goals in the NFL until he was 48, that Gordie Howe played professional hockey until he was 51, that tennis great Billie Jean King attempted a comeback in her late thirties, and, more recently, Michael Jordan was a star on the basketball court playing with guys half his age, most Olympic athletes are in their teens or twenties and are considered old once they hit their thirties.

For most people, reflexes, strength, and speed diminish after their teens or twenties. Exercising regularly, eating sensibly, and staying away from nicotine and alcohol certainly help, but only to an extent. There is no way to fend off the aging process forever, despite the type of advertisement that is becoming increasingly common: "What if we told you that human aging is not a natural consequence of life, but a disease that can be treated?" (Ad for Longevity Dietary Supplement, Lifestyle Fascination catalog, Spring 2001, p. 24.) Baby boomers are finding that growing old is difficult to accept.

Metabolic rates decline about 2 percent per decade in adult life, and both women and men gain weight as they age. At midlife, women gain more weight than men because menopause itself lowers resting metabolic rate (Barbach, 2000, p. 113). Both men and women at midlife find it easy to put on weight and hard to take it off. A woman I interviewed expressed both anger and sorrow:

> This weight thing is a bummer. I've exercised my whole life and have always been in great shape. But in the last five years I've gained 12 pounds that I can't do anything about. Not only am I bigger, but also flabbier. I do more bicep and tricep exercises than Mr America, yet my upper arms get flabbier and flabbier. I'm ashamed to wave hello or goodbye to anyone if my arms are exposed. I exercise almost every day, I eat little or no fat, yet there it is. I thought I would get some good advice from my doctor. I was flabbergasted to hear her say, 'Can't help you. I have the same problem myself, as do most of my patients. God is either a misogynist or has a terrible sense of humor. If you find something that helps, please let me know.' Now that's really terrific, I should let her know!

A redistribution of fatty tissues occurs for both sexes at midlife. This results in increased body weight and changes in girth, a process that typically begins earlier than one would hope for, as early as the mid-20s, and continues through the mid-50s. Weight gain around menopause is particularly rapid for women. Men become more apple-shaped, with a tire around the middle, whereas women become more pear-shaped, with extra weight distributed on the hips, buttocks, and stomach area (Daniluk, 1998, p. 247).

Anaerobic and aerobic capacity steadily decline with age. Between the ages of 40 and 70, the average loss of muscular strength is 10 to 20 percent. Between 70 and 80, the loss is much greater. Something most of us don't give much thought to is bone strength. Yet it is important. During adulthood bone strength declines, with the period of maximum loss occurring between the ages of 50 and 70. The result is a diminished capacity of our bones to withstand pressure and a greater vulnerability to fracture (Whitbourne, 1999, p. 96). Accompanying loss of bone strength are decreases in joint functioning. Virtually every component of our joints loses strength over the adult years (ibid). Doing things we took for granted when we were younger becomes more difficult, more energy draining, and less effective (Whitbourne, 1999).

Our immune system also deteriorates with age. This is an important change because it means we are more susceptible to illness and that recovery and recuperation are more difficult. Pneumonia is a good example. It can affect anyone of any age. But in young people, it's usually not a big deal. Recovery is virtually assured. Yet pneumonia is one of the most common causes of death in the later years. The older body simply can't fight it off.

Another unpleasant change: We tire more easily and can't do all the things we did, or as easily, as 10 years earlier. We aren't as strong or as fast, and it takes longer to heal from injury. A strain or sprain that in our younger days would have resolved in a few hours or days now can take a week or more to get over. Needless to say, the more down-time you have due to even minor ailments, the less you may desire sex. Many respondents noted that they simply don't have the energy they used to have; this may be an important reason that sexual frequency declines with age. A 62-year-old man noted: "I don't have as much energy for as many things as I used to and this has definitely cut into the amount of sex we have. It used to be that a night out at the symphony or movies was great foreplay. Now it just uses me up and I'm sexually useless until I get some sleep. Likewise, a busy day at work didn't make that much difference when I was younger. Now it's likely to drain me." Which reminds me of a joke that came via the Internet the other day: Midlife woman: "Honey, let's go upstairs and make love." Midlife man: "Sorry, I can only do one or the other." Some of my interviewees, and clients as well, sheepishly admitted that they had started taking naps in the afternoon. Of course, the depletion of energy and time can come from many sources, not all of them having to do with the body getting older. One man in his mid-50s, for example, noted that his sexual desire has decreased because of the energy and time involved in caring for college-age children as well as infirm parents. As a result, he says, "We actually have less time to ourselves and more responsibilities, and we often feel less sexual or even awake."

For many people, the first sign of aging is in the eyes or, more precisely, a decreasing ability to see things up close. This change, called presbyopia by vision experts, usually starts around age 40 and is inevitable and universal. Everyone gets it and there's no cure except to use reading glasses. The cause of presbyopia is the stiffening of the parts of the eye that help us focus. One day you realize you can't read the small print on a food package at the market, or you have trouble with a map or looking up a number in the phone book. At first you try to deal with it by holding the object further away and that works for a while, but then you have to hold it so far away that the print is too small to see. Can't see near, can't see far. Congratulations! You and your youth have gotten divorced and there's no way back.

Our skin undergoes changes too. The supporting fibers under the skin start to break down as the years go by, with the result that the skin becomes less elastic and starts wrinkling and, well, sort of drooping in some places. And we are all familiar with the double standard: wrinkles and gray hair make a man look distinguished; they make a woman look old. Of special concern to many women, as I've already mentioned, is what happens to their upper arms. It's a phenomenon that Joan Rivers once described as "flesh dangling from [one's] arms and wafting in the wind like pink sails" (Rivers, 1999, p. 37). A woman who sells women's clothes in a department store says it's virtually impossible to sell a sleeveless or shortsleeve shirt or blouse to a woman over 40, or even 35, unless the item is going to be worn underneath something else with long sleeves. Although nothing can prevent skin from wrinkling, losing elasticity, and drooping, staying out of the sun and not smoking can mitigate and slow the damage.

Then there's the issue of hair. Many men start losing their hair quite early and many men are balding by the time they reach their 40s or 50s. Balding or not, gray hairs make their appearance, hair starts appearing in places we'd rather it didn't. We find stray hairs, or even whole bushes, growing in our nose and ears. But men are not the only ones with hair issues in mid life. Women's hair also turns grey, and thins, especially on the head and pubic area, and, for some women, starts to fall out. Around the menopause or within the years afterward, many women may find more or new hair on their upper lips, chins, or chests. Even teeth come into the picture or, more accurately, drop out of the picture. A great many Americans lose teeth as they age. The usual causes are cavities, periodontal disease, and accidents. According to an article in *The New York Times* citing statistics from the Centers for Disease Control, by age 17, seven percent of people in the US have lost at least one permanent tooth among adults 35 to 44, whereas 69 percent have lost at least one permanent tooth by age 50. Americans have lost an average of twelve teeth (including wisdom teeth) between ages 65–74 and 26 percent have lost all their teeth (Julie Bain, "Goodbye, Dentures: Improved Dental Implants Gaining Favor," *NY Times*, Tues, Sept 11, 2001, p. D5). Most of the losses are preventable if only people would take better care of their gums and teeth. Nonetheless these are the current statistics.

It shouldn't come as any surprise that the bottom line, our feet, are also affected by aging. It is estimated that by the time we reach 50, we've walked 75,000 miles, about three times around the planet. And it shows. According to a survey by the American Podiatric Medical Association, more than 40 percent of Americans thought occasional foot pain was normal. Problems like corns and bunions typically surface at midlife and later and they can literally force us off our feet ("Best Feet Forward", *Newsweek*, Sept 10, 2001, p. 70). One of my respondents reported that at age 53, her bunions finally defeated her and she had to submit to surgery. After years of wearing high-heel shoes, which her doctor kept warning her about, the pain became excruciating. She could barely walk a city block, let alone the 5 and 10 mile hikes she loved. The surgery was successful and after two weeks of recuperation, she was almost as good as new. She's now able to do her long hikes without foot pain. And she threw out all of her high heel shoes.

There is one other change, or more accurately a sense about the changes that are upon us that should be mentioned. Many people at midlife—some of whom have experienced only some of the physical alterations noted in the last few pages and some of whom have experienced these changes plus sexual changes (to which we turn in a moment) and/or the diseases and conditions addressed in the next chapter—have a clear sense that their bodies have betrayed them. Time and again, I heard the same litany from my respondents, including from the Lovers: "It's really sad. I was so healthy, vibrant, and energetic. And then it's like my body betrayed me or abandoned me."

The various physical changes of midlife can and do affect people's sense of their sexuality, and women seem much more sensitive to these changes than men. For example, a study done in 1991 found that only one-sixth of the men felt their weight gain had negatively affected their sex lives, whereas nearly half of the women did (Barbach, 2000, p. 112). And that's only one variable among many.

There's no doubt that the physical changes of midlife preoccupy many women. They report feeling "invisible" because men no longer look at them as sexual beings. According to two researchers: "Middle-aged women see themselves as less attractive than do any other age group" (Quoted in Daniluk, 1998, p. 259). Particularly distasteful to these women are increased weight, flabby skin and musculature, sagging breasts and buttocks, wrinkles, and increased skin pigmentation. It often takes a period of several years for a woman to come to terms with her new body. As a woman nearing 60 put it, "I have an acute awareness of gravity. Things are not where they once were. This is a shock to me, that my breasts are lower down and hips wider out. It's a very odd experience to look at my own body."

In truth, most people agree that older bodies, female and male alike, are not as attractive as younger ones. The standard of physical beauty and sexiness in our culture and almost all cultures has been youth. Yet it's also true that older bodies can be attractive in their own ways. I'm not referring here to people whose attractiveness is based on their not looking their chronological ages, but rather to women and men who look pretty much as they should at their age. A large majority of the older people I've worked with over the years, and also the ones I interviewed, can acknowledge what they don't especially like about their own and their partner's bodies, but still manage to retain their sexual appetites and follow through on them. In other words, given time, the vast majority of people do accept their new bodies and get on with their lives.

In fact, lest I give the wrong impression, despite all the changes just noted, considerable research shows that many postmenopausal women report "feeling better, more confident, calmer, and freer than they did before menopause" (Daniluk, 1998, p. 258). They are relieved and happy to be free of periods and the possibility of conception. Contrary to some silly theorizing in the past, women welcome their empty nests; now that their children are gone they realize they can focus on their relationships, work, and old or new hobbies. And many of these women also report being more connected to their sexuality than ever before (Daniluk, 1998, p. 262).

The Impact of Age on Sexuality

Sexual desire and frequency decreases

Research has consistently demonstrated a decline in sexual desire for men and women as they age. Let's look at some findings from a recent study on sexual frequency and increasing age for more than 13,000 married couples. Sexual intercourse took place at least once a month according to age as follows:

96 percent of those aged 19–24
92 percent of those aged 30–34
83 percent of those aged 50–54
57 percent of those aged 65–69
27 percent of those aged 75 and over

Health problems have something to do with the decline, but there was a decreased frequency reported even for couples where both partners are healthy. I should note that 6.75 percent of the couples aged 75 and over were actually still having sex an average of three times a month. These are probably 'Lovers', the same kind of sexually proficient couples I came across researching this book (Call *et al*, cited in Hillman, 2000, pp. 23–24).

For men, we see a gradual yet fairly consistent decrease in desire for sexual arousal and sexual activity (Schiavi, 1999, p. 43). And a small percentage of men experience a veritable nose dive at some point as they age. Not only do men desire sex less as they age, but they also think and dream less about sex and find it more difficult to become sexually interested.

Women may also experience a gradual decline in interest and activity over time. One woman describes it this way: "I was married when I was 40 and the sex wasn't that great, but we had more of it than I'm having now. The sex currently is terrific, but I don't need to have it more than once or twice a week." Noteworthy, however, is that for many women, a precipitous drop occurs around menopause. In some women, sexual thoughts and fantasies disappear and there's no desire to masturbate.

There seem to be a number of common reasons for a loss of sexual libido for both men and women, and the two prevalent ones are problems in the relationship outside the bedroom and hormones. Let's take hormones first.

It appears that the hormone responsible for sexual desire is testosterone. Men experience a gradual decrease in testosterone production that begins around age 50. The lower the amount of available (also called circulating or free) testosterone, the lower the level of desire (Leiblum & Seagraves, 2000, p. 438). Women also encounter a decrease in testosterone, and the drop can be rather dramatic around menopause. And even though women have less testosterone to begin with, a drop in the usual level is what appears to be responsible for the lowered libido.

Testosterone supplementation is available for men and women by prescription in the form of pills, injections, and gel. For men, patches that adhere to the scrotum are also available. If lowered libido is due to low testosterone, the results can be dramatic when the man or woman is given extra doses of the hormone. Some who haven't wanted sex in a year or more suddenly can't get enough. But there is danger in using testosterone if the body already has as much as it needs; it can cause liver damage, acne, and irritability or aggressiveness. In men, it can also accelerate the growth of prostate cancer. If you believe you are deficient in testosterone—if your desire is close to zero or has taken an inexplicably dramatic decline—you should consult with your physician.

As if lowered testosterone levels were not problematic enough, women also have to contend with symptoms of lowered estrogen around menopause: hot flashes, headaches, and fatigue can have a direct impact on sexual desire. Desire usually returns to normal level when the woman is postmenopausal. Several women I interviewed reported that dealing with the symptoms of the menopause was so exhausting, they didn't even think of sex for months, but that now their desire is back on track. Other women had different responses. For instance, "Although I was going nuts with hot flushes and cold flashes and all sorts of mysterious maladies, I still wanted sex and got it as often as my partner was interested. I guess there's almost nothing that gets in the way of my desire."

Estrogen can reduce hot flushes and other discomforts and thereby increase sexual interest. However, in some cases the added estrogen competes with free testosterone and ends up actually decreasing desire. Getting this hormonal balance right can be pretty tricky business even if you ignore the fact that estrogen can have some long-term negative side effects.

If hormones are not the problem, a relationship filled with acrimony, strife, or just plain boredom can dampen if not kill sexual desire outright. So can a relationship fraught with sexual problems or unsatisfying sex in the past. When an unhappy relationship or unresolved sexual issues are responsible for a lack of libido, we often see sexual interest alive and well elsewhere, but not directed at the partner. Men and women may masturbate or turn to sexual affairs. Men (more often than women) also may seek out prostitutes or cruise the Internet.

However, for many men and women the sex drive does not disappear at any age. Interest has been documented in men between the ages of 80 and 100. It's just not as frequent or urgent as it was in earlier years. Here's how one man in his late 50s with an enlarged prostate describes the changes: "Fantasies that used to be a turn on are now bland and sort of blah. I can go much longer without sex or thinking about sex. Certainly the old jokes about guys who only think about sex applied to me in my younger years. But these days I can go a long time, several weeks even, without even thinking about or desiring sex. It's hard to figure out if this is all due to age or if my prostate discomfort also has something to do with it."

The main exception to the rule of decreased desire with age is when a new partner comes into the picture. A man or woman who is involved with a new lover after the death or divorce of the former partner is likely to find that the level of desire is more like it was in his or her 30s or 40s, at least for a while. But after a few weeks or months, when the 'newness' wears off, desire usually diminishes. A similar phenomenon is also manifest in couples who rekindle the romantic/sexual side of long relationships after a period of neglect. After the last child leaves home, or upon retirement or some other milepost, some couples decide to put more energy into their relationship and sex life. This often results in increased desire, at least for a while.

For those couples who are interested, there are ways of generating more long-lasting changes in erotic desire and activity. These include making the relationship as close, romantic, and sexy as possible, which often means resolving or letting go of hurts and resentments; making the sexual setting as inviting as possible, either by spiffing up the usual place of lovemaking or by spending more time in exotic settings (remembering that at any age, sex tends to be more frequent away from home); making sure each partner is getting what they need to make sex as appealing and satisfying as possible; and experimenting with different positions, locations, times, and also with erotica, sexual toys, and fantasy.

Although I have no proof, I wonder about the role of obesity in lessening desire and frequency. America is perhaps as much the land of the fat as it is the land of the free. In recent years, there has been a fantastic rise in the number of women and men who are, by any reasonable standards, fat. The best estimates I could find suggest that about a third of adults are obese. I am not talking about five, ten, or even twenty extra pounds. I'm talking significantly more. Excess poundage takes a lot of energy to move around. Say a woman or man should weigh around 160. If the person actually weighed 300 pounds, it's as though he or she is carrying around a 140-pound backpack or a whole other person. Do you have a sense of how tired that would make you? And that's exactly what is involved when a person is that much overweight. When our bodies are younger and stronger, and our sexual drives are much stronger, this burden is easier to overcome. But as we move into middle and older age, when energy is already being depleted in many ways, the excess weight gets progressively more difficult to handle. A number of the people I interviewed spontaneously stated that they thought they would have sex more often if they lost weight. It's an idea worth considering.

As with all changes associated with aging, there is tremendous variability when it comes to sexual desire. Some report only a small loss of interest and some deny any loss of interest well into their 60s and 70s. It is crucial to keep the variability in mind. But when thinking about decreased desire, it is also important to consider all factors. The level of desire can be influenced by many things—hormones, a boring sex life, a distressed relationship, depression, work or other stresses, the general state of your health, and the chemicals (prescribed or not, legal or not) that you are ingesting.

Men

Changes in penile functioning
There's no question that the penis, like the rest of the body, becomes less exuberant and active as the years go by. More specifically …

Fewer and less rigid sleeping erections
Research on healthy men by Raul Schiavi at the Mt Sinai School of Medicine in New York has shown that we have fewer night-time erections (the ones like you see in the morning on awakening) and they are much less rigid than before. These erections are good indicators of the state of our sexual plumbing.

Takes more to get an erection during sex

In our younger years, the penis literally jumped up ready for action at the slightest provocation. Just seeing our partner, or any other attractive woman, or holding or kissing her, was enough to cause an erection. But as the years go by, this happens less and less. Often, by middle age, a man won't get an erection without direct stimulation. Seeing and kissing are no longer enough. As Masters & Johnson put it: "Generally, the older the male is, the longer it takes to achieve full penile erection, regardless of the effectiveness of the stimulative techniques employed." (Masters & Johnson, 1966, p. 251)

And sometimes even good stimulation by self or partner is not sufficient. The best study ever done on the subject of aging and erections demonstrated that 51 percent of men over the age of 50 reported some level of difficulty attaining or maintaining erections. (McKinlay & Feldman, 1994) This is just a normal part of aging and nothing to get upset about unless, of course, it takes you by surprise.

I was consulted by a 53-year-old man with erection problems. He was a very strong-willed independent man who liked to take charge and feel in control of everything that happened to him. Although he had been married twice, and had had a number of relationships between the marriages, he had very little experience with a woman stimulating his penis manually or orally. He hadn't needed it. As he put it, "I'd be stiff from the get-go. No point wasting time playing with me. The real issue was me stimulating her so she'd want me to put it in her." But a few years ago, this pattern stopped working and he started having problems gaining an erection. When I suggested he ask his partner for a penile massage, he was taken aback. He didn't like the idea one bit because, as he whispered sadly, "It makes me feel old. I exercise a lot, eat right, and am in great shape. Now you're telling me that despite all that, I'm aging. That's not easy to take."

Easy to take it may not be, but it is real. Fortunately, this man stayed in therapy long enough to become more open to his situation and to accept direct stimulation from his partner, which is all he needed to have better erections.

Another man in his mid-50s says: "My reaction time is slower. I'm not as instantaneously aroused now as I was 10–15 years ago. Takes longer to get an erection. After a busy day at the office, I tend to be less interested in sex and find it difficult to perform. I don't seem to be able to switch gears as quickly as I used to from a busy day at work to sex at home. But when we've had a good day or evening together, my response is a lot quicker. My wife's changes parallel mine. When she's had a hard day at work, or when the two of us have a bad day, it's difficult for her to get in the mood. It takes her longer to get aroused and to climax."

One reason that men take longer to get erections in the mature years may be that penises becomes less sensitive to stimulation with age. Although some diseases, such as diabetes, can also have this effect, the simple fact of growing older makes its own contribution. This generally means that new kinds of stimulation, firmer stimulation, or longer periods of stimulation may be required.

Erections not as rigid

For the adolescent to 25-year-old, the penis often feels and is described as being rock-hard. But erections this rigid are not so common in later years. The erections are usually serviceable—that is, capable of vaginal penetration and of giving pleasure to all parties involved—but their less than baseball bat rigidity worries some men unnecessarily. And, unfortunately, their concern often makes matters worse. The trick, of course, is to accept that although your penis is no longer as hard as it once was, it's still capable of giving you and your partner a good time.

Some men notice and worry about the angle of erection. The erection that in younger years pointed up may now just stick straight out; the one that in previous times stuck straight out may now, even though relatively rigid, point slightly down. In most cases, these are just normal changes and nothing to get nervous about. Once again I note the variability among men. For example, here is the account of a man almost 70 years old to my question about changes in penile functioning over the years: "Not much has changed although it probably doesn't throb as much as it used to. I've been jogging since the late 1960s and I think that has a lot to do with how I am. Also, at that time, I cut my weight down and stopped smoking."

On the other hand, there were men in their 40s and 50s who reported that erections were not as rigid as when they were younger and that they took significantly more time to get hard. One man in his middle 50s said this: "For several years I've noticed that I have fewer morning erections and, whether morning or night, my erections aren't as strong as they used to be." Upon noticing these changes, some men decide they're over the hill as far as sex goes or that they need some help. Getting help is realistic for some, but for others all that's needed is the understanding that just because something isn't the way it was 20, 30, or 40 years ago doesn't mean you can't use and enjoy it. A raging erection that points at the ceiling and that won't quit is not necessary for good sex. After all, many men in their 60s and 70s enjoy walking, jogging, golfing, and dancing even though they can't move as fast or as far as they did when they were younger. The senior penis can still give and take pleasure, even if some of the rules have changed.

Time between erections increases

Older erections are easier to lose than younger ones and after one is lost, for any reason including orgasm, it may take much longer to have another one. If there has been orgasm, it may take many hours, even a day or two, before the man is capable of having another erection. In Masters and Johnson's terminology, the refractory period lengthens. Once again, this is not a matter for concern, just the effects of aging.

Here's how one man in his 60s describes the changes in his penis: "It must have been about February or March of 1993; we were in Florida for a solid week of recreation. I had been looking forward to it because vacations have always been good for us sexually. During that week I realized for the first time that my potency was significantly less than what it had been. My erections were clearly weaker, more wobbly, and I lost more of them. Regaining them took lots of time and stimulation. Several times we just had to give up and go on to other things. It was a difficult week. I would say that ever since then, over the past five years, there has been a decline and a devolution. There have been times that I've thought, oh boy! I'm right back to normal. Wow. I'm like I was when I was 20 or something. But those are short-lived. I would say if we drew a graph, it would go down, down, down, down. So, I'm now ready for Viagra. I'm going to get a barrel of it."

The Viagra revolution

It used to be that age-related changes in penile functioning largely dictated the content of sexuality at midlife and afterwards. Many couples simply gave up on sex as soon as the man started having difficulties with getting or keeping erections. But our ideas and practices are changing. One reason is that in recent years it has become easier to think and talk about sex and as a result more and more people understand that a rock-hard, easy-to-get-and-maintain erection is not absolutely necessary for good sex. A second reason is the advent of Viagra, which for many men largely overcomes age-related change in penile functioning. There is no doubt that this little blue pill has been a godsend for many men and their partners. A large majority of mature men with erection problems have found that taking the pill as prescribed results in quite serviceable erections. And compared to most other 'miracle' drugs—the modern antidepressants (Prozac-style SSRIs) for example—the side effects are relatively few and are easily handled. For instance, men who get headaches from taking Viagra can prevent them by taking an aspirin or Tylenol at the same time as they take the pill. For those whom Viagra does not help, there are also penile injections, and a host of new chemical helpers on the way—pills, patches, gels, and inhalants—that can result in more frequent and harder erections.

Although Viagra has its critics—whose main complaint seems to be that it is a part of medicalization of sexuality—as a therapist, I have been quite pleased to have it available. Viagra is often not useful when relationship problems are at the foundation of a lack of desire or performance—and especially for the woman who actually welcomes her husband's diminished capacity. But for many older men and couples it is a miracle.

The need to ejaculate is less urgent

As men age, the need for orgasm is less pronounced, and this may be one reason why frequency decreases; after all, the desire to have an orgasm is one of the main motivators for men to pursue sex. In addition, the force of the ejaculation is less, as is the amount ejaculated. Penises at this age often take longer to ejaculate and don't need to ejaculate in every sexual encounter. Every second or third time is fine. The good news here is that because of the general slowing down of things, premature ejaculation is usually cured by Mother Nature herself. Men who were quick on the trigger in their youth now find they can take their time and enjoy the scenery, and this is often a change much welcomed by their partners.

Ejaculation becomes less powerful. Semen may seem to seep out instead of shooting out. And, as already noted, once a 50ish, 60ish, or 70ish-year-old penis ejaculates, it may be a day or more before it can get hard again.

There has not been much research on the intensity or pleasure of orgasm, but it is a question I asked my interviewees. Most of my respondents reported little change, but some men did note a decrease in penile sensitivity and also a decrease in orgasmic intensity; for example, a man in his late 60s said, "My whole apparatus seems less sensitive than it used to be. Certainly it takes longer to orgasm and there's less intensity, less pleasure. It feels like there is a much higher threshold." Some men noted only very small changes; for instance, "It's not quite as nerve tingling as it was in earlier years, but it is still extremely pleasurable." The largest number of men said it was about the same as before. One man in his late 50s reported fewer morning erections and less rigid erections at any time. Nonetheless, this is what he said when asked about changes in his orgasms: "That's the good part, no changes at all. They're still very intense." Another man: "Feels just as intense and just as good. Praise the Lord for that."

The changes I've described gradually continue until the end of life. Like the rest of physical functioning, the erection and ejaculatory processes become less efficient. But the penis and the rest of the body *never* lose their capacity for pleasure. There are men in their 70s, 80s, and 90s who enjoy sex, and I know because I interviewed a number of them.

The big problem for penises lies in our outlandish expectations. The adolescent penis is the one that's idealized and idolized, and it's also the first penis males have sexual experience with. Everyone, especially men, expect penises of any age to act like they do during adolescence.

In other areas we don't have these outrageous expectations. When it's old timer's day in baseball, we don't expect the stars of yesterday to hit and run and pitch the way they did before. And we don't expect a 40-year-old man to run as fast as he did when he won the 100-meter race in the Olympics. But almost every man expects his penis to behave the way it did when he was 17 years old.

If we can learn to accept the penis that we now have, meet its needs, and like and enjoy it for what it is, we can give and receive erotic pleasure as much as we want and for as long as we want.

Now for another piece of good news.

Satisfaction with sex does not change with age

Despite all of the physical changes noted thus far, research has found that as long as men are having reasonably frequent sex with a partner, most men seem satisfied with their sex lives. Herewith the conclusions from the two best studies: "Despite the marked decline in actual events and behavior and in subjective aspects of sexuality, men in their sixties reported levels of satisfaction with their sex life and partners at about the same level as younger men ..." (McKinlay & Feldman, 1994, p. 272). "The degree of satisfaction with the men's own sexual functioning or enjoyment of marital sexuality did not change with age" (Schiavi, 1999, p. 44).

This is exactly what I found in my interviews. Even men who reported less rigid erections, who needed more stimulation or time to get erect, or had to take Viagra to stay erect, maintained that sex was as good or better than ever. For example, a man in his 80s: "It's less wild, but no less good." A number of other men also noted that although sexual activity was less gymnastic or experimental than in previous years, it was still "ecstatic", "wonderful", "feels as good as ever", "more mellow more loving, all in all a bit better".

One man makes an interesting comparison between sex at age 40 and the present. He says the quality of sex between the two ages is different.

> I was dating then and the sex was more physical and animalistic, and less personal. If I had to pick, I would choose the kind of sex I have now because there's a lot of personal feeling and caring in it as well as the physical side.

In Part 2, we will see how older men who have wonderful sex cope with age-related changes, both with and without chemical aids.

Women

The alert reader will soon notice that this section is shorter than the one on men and may feel that I, being a man, am biased toward my sex. Fear not. The fact is that no matter what horrors you may have read about concerning the negative effects of the menopause and the years after on female sexuality, women's sexuality is generally much less affected by the aging process than men's. For instance, more than 50 percent of menopausal women report no decrease at all in sexual desire, and fewer than 20 percent report a significant decrease.

As might be expected from the discussion on men, in women, breast engorgement and nipple erection are less pronounced as the years go by. Vaginal secretions are decreased, as is clitoral engorgement.

Intercourse can become painful

Many women at midlife, because of declining estrogen levels, have reduced blood flow to the vagina. This results in less vaginal lubrication than previously and also an increased amount of time and stimulation needed to become lubricated. Another consequence of declining estrogen levels is a loss of elasticity and a thinning of the vaginal lining. The vagina also shrinks in size. The result of all the changes can be painful intercourse. Over the counter lubricants and hormone replacement are the usual remedies and they work quite well. But studies have shown that equally important to vaginal health is regular exercise, meaning sexual activity, with or without a partner. From my therapy practice, I can report that regular exercise of the vagina, especially with something inside of it (penis, vibrator, plastic dildo, or a penis-sized carrot, zuchinni, or similar vegetable) can make a difference in keeping the vagina lubricated and walls supple. (Don't laugh. The veggies work as well as dildos and vibrators. Besides, they're organic.) There really is a use it or lose it phenomenon. A number of women in my practice, as well as among my respondents, reported that when sex was infrequent, for whatever reasons, they had a number of problems. With more frequent sex, of whatever kind, the problems typically lessened in quantity and severity.

For some women, however, intercourse still hurts sometimes. Couples with this situation have to be much more careful about which positions are used and be very attentive to the effects of insertion and thrusting. Some will have intercourse less frequently and rely more on clitoral stimulation for the woman's enjoyment.

Aside from having sex on the regular basis, many of the problems women experience can be alleviated with estrogen, vaginal cream, or hormone replacement therapy (HRT). HRT usually refers to taking estrogen and progesterone (if you have a uterus) in pill form. It has been shown in many studies to be effective in combating hot flushes, mood swings, and painful intercourse. As usual, there is a risk of side-effects, everything from sore breasts, serious depression, and possibly breast cancer. It can also lower libido. The risks and benefits have to be carefully evaluated and although not every woman needs additional estrogen, I've been involved in a number of cases where it has been very helpful. Intercourse and the whole sexual experience became much more pleasurable with the fear of pain removed.

Taking longer to get aroused and reach orgasm

This is actually a controversial point. Although there is no doubt that some women find that it takes longer than previously to get physically aroused and there may be a bit more difficulty getting to orgasm, it's by no means clear how many women are so affected. As with men, we see variability. And for those who do have problems, relationship problems and lowered levels of testosterone are frequently the culprits.

Most of the Lovers I interviewed reported that getting excited and reaching orgasm remained about the same as in earlier years. Their orgasms were as intense as before or more so, and at least as easy to get to. One study found that the frequency of orgasm for sexually active women *increased in each decade of life through the 70s* (Starr & Weiner, 1981). Even for those for whom this is not the case, the changes are generally not considered significant and do not necessarily diminish sexual enjoyment. In fact, while some women report less intense orgasms in later life, they often describe them as gentler, sexier, and sweeter.

A woman's capacity for multiple orgasm is typically not affected by menopause or aging. A number of women I interviewed spontaneously reported having multiple orgasms in their 50s, 60s, and 70s. If they had such orgasms in youth, they continued having them. A very small number discovered multiple climaxes after menopause.

This is one area where women have it all over men. As we have noted, with age, men want and have fewer orgasms. After each, the time required for the man to be able to function again gets longer. Women do not experience such a limitation. If they've had strings of orgasms earlier in life, they can continue to do so regardless of how old they are.

And here's the same bit of good news we found for men.

Satisfaction with sex does not change with age

Despite the physical changes that occur in aging women, many women report the same degree of sexual pleasure and satisfaction. A number of studies have found that many older women say their sexual pleasure had either stayed the same with the passing years or had even increased (Hite, 1976; Brecher, 1984; Starr & Weiner, 1981). Among the Lovers, all of them reported that their sexual pleasure had either increased over time or stayed about the same.

As far as menopause is concerned, it goes both ways. While for some women it does result in a decline of libido, clearly many other women find it liberating. Without having to worry about conception and contraception, some of them, for the first time in their lives, find their sexual wings.

One woman I talked to belonged to this group. For over 25 years of marriage, she enjoyed the closeness of sex when she wasn't concerned about getting pregnant but never understood what all the excitement was about. At the age of 52, she started reading about sex and discovered that she'd never had an orgasm. Maybe, she thought, she had been missing something. Her husband was surprised by her new interest; he had largely given up on sex because she wasn't a very exciting partner. But together they read, had a few sessions with a therapist, and explored. She had her first orgasm a month later. She and her husband have had their best sex over the last 10 years. Her only regret, she said, was that she didn't get the information years earlier.

The biggest problem for many women over 50 or 60 has little to do with the physical changes they experience and far more to do with the shortage of available men. Some women can't find a man at all, and some have a man who isn't much interested in sex. Increasing numbers of these women are turning to masturbation as a means of sexual pleasure, and there's nothing wrong with that. Of course if the problem is that she's interested and he's not and they're both willing to embark on some therapy, something may be able to be done about it.

So there you have it. The general and specific sexual changes that are normal aspects of aging for all of us. I hope you agree with me that, although things do change, the changes do not have to be devastating or even far-reaching. It's possible to accept them without panic or anxiety, possible to accommodate to them, and possible to have bonding and enjoyable sex in their presence. There's no doubt that aging brings physical changes almost all of us would rather not have, but so far there is no alternative. As a brilliant person once said, the best revenge is living well. Why not?

Chapter 3

Challenges of Midlife Sexuality, Medical and Otherwise

Several years before I had thought of writing this book, I met a fifty-two-year old woman who had many health problems, including chronic fatigue syndrome, severe osteoporosis and arthritis. She was easy to be with and I felt increasingly comfortable asking questions about her situation. I didn't want to be intrusive, but at the same time I was curious what her life was like, so at one point I asked for a summary. Her reply:

> I'm of two minds on this. On the one hand, I have a good life. My children are grown up and doing well. I did a good job with them. And my marriage is terrific, far better than I expected and far better than I see around me. Much to my surprise, the sex has remained good despite the many years together and my medical problems. I'm a sexy, sexually fulfilled midlife person, and damned proud of it!

But there are days, today is one of them, when I feel sorry for myself and focus on the other side, the one that feels victimized because things are being taken away from me. Don't take this the wrong way, but I had a very nice, well-conditioned body, and that's gone. Because of my constant pain and all the drugs I've taken, I haven't been able to do much exercise and it shows. I had boundless energy; now I have to limit the number of phone calls I take or make in a day. And I used to love my karate practice. Nothing fancy—I never thought I was going to be the next Bruce Lee—but a soon-to-be-middle-aged woman learning the discipline of this incredible martial art. I was getting good. I had a brown belt and was slowly working my way to black. I know it's hard for others to understand, but I loved it all. I was so jazzed by the kicking and punching, sparring and practice, I'd be on a high for hours afterward. I'd give anything to be able to practice again, but I doubt I ever will. I'm so weak and my back and neck are so bad that I can barely walk a few blocks without serious pain. To me it's very sad; all the things I once loved and that are no longer possible.

I'm looking forward to tomorrow when I'll probably be feeling better about myself and will be more focused on the good things I have and am a part of.

Midlife and beyond is the time of disease and disability, of things no longer possible. While it's true that many mature men and women are healthy and without physical impairment, and while it is true that we are living longer and healthier lives than any generation before in human history, it is also true that with every passing year, women and men are more likely to suffer from heart disease, various cancers, arthritis, diabetes, osteoporosis, lower back pain, and other afflictions. If you have reached or passed your 45th birthday, you probably already have personal or vicarious examples of this phenomenon. Either you or someone you know has almost certainly been affected by one or more of these conditions. Most of these conditions have sexual consequences and so do many of the treatments, whether surgery or medications.

If you're the kind of person who prefers not to hear bad news, you may want to skip the rest of this chapter. Although in a later chapter I give examples of Lovers living high-quality lives despite these afflictions, here I simply report the typical consequences of the common ailments of the middle and later years. It may not be the kind of thing you want to read. On the other hand, if you're like me and prefer to hear all the news, good and bad, please read on.

In an important way, this chapter is a continuation of the previous one on normal physical changes due to aging. It is typical for those over 45 years old to have one or more of the diseases and disabilities discussed herein. There is nothing unnatural or unusual in this. Maturity goes hand in hand with deterioration of the physical body. Keep in mind then that the conditions addressed in this chapter are nothing unusual, just what happens sooner or later to all of us as we age. And it's not just a matter of bad habits. A few years ago, the mother of a good friend died from lung cancer. She had never had a cigarette in her life. And she's not the only one. There was vast consternation among exercisers years ago when Jim Fixx, the man who had almost single-handedly popularized jogging for adults, died of a heart attack after one of his runs. He was only 52. Matures, who are in great condition from regular exercise and healthy living, get sick and die all the time. One would be hard put to say what they could have done differently to extend their health and lives.

Although we cry out in sadness, anger, and fear when we learn that we or someone close is diagnosed with cancer, stroke, or any number of other life-threatening illnesses, it is probably the case that 100 or even 50 years ago that person wouldn't have lived long enough to have that particular malady. They would have been struck down years earlier. The added years are evidence of the incredible progress of public health measures, greater general knowledge of health and disease, and medical technology. Yet at some point the illnesses still occur and people still die.

Aging and disease

The idea is simply put: the older we get, the more diseases and health problems we have. The correlation is astounding. For example, heart disease is the major killer of both men and women. Herewith the death rates for heart disease at different ages:

	Death rate per 100,000 population	
Age:	**Women**	**Men**
15–24 years	2.4	3.6
25–44 years	11.4	28.1
45–64 years	105.3	264.9
65 and over	1,667.1	1,944.4

(Statistical Abstract of the US, 120th Edition, Hoover's Business Press, 2001, p. 93)

The largest increase for men occurs from the years of 25 to 44 to the midlife years of 45 to 64, a more than nine times jump. Women experience an even larger increase from midlife to old age, during which they lose their hormonal protection against heart disease.

Disability also increases with age, disability defined as limits in any activities because of impairments or health problems, or needing special equipment such as a walker or help from others to get around. Here, from a recent report from the Centers For Disease Control, is the prevalence of disability among women and men respondents taken together at different ages:

18 to 44	9.7 percent
45 to 64	22.1 percent
65 and older	30.8 percent

(MMWR August 11, 2000)

Put differently, more than a fifth of men and women in midlife are disabled; that becomes almost a third in old age. This is good news for the majority who are not disabled, but it does mean that significant numbers of men and women suffer from one kind of disability or another, which can make it difficult to maneuver during sex and can also drain energy that might have been available for sex in doing ordinary daily chores. Disease and disabilities, once relative strangers, become frequent visitors, regular parts of our daily lives. And they do not come alone. Instead, they come with their associates—hassle, pain, and drugs—each of these has its own set of problems.

The hassle factor

When you're ill and disabled, the accommodations one has to make are both time-consuming and energy-sapping. The busy work of being unwell, this is what I call the hassle factor. Put bluntly, daily life becomes much more of a drag. One woman I talked to, a relatively young 52 years old, has to spend 45 minutes every morning doing stretching exercises; otherwise, she risks serious back pain during the rest of the day. No big deal, you say, it's just 45 minutes. But think: this time is no longer available for sleeping, showering and dressing, making phone calls, answering e-mail, eating breakfast, getting to work, or making love. Forty-five minutes each morning, three-quarters of an hour previously free for other matters, is no longer available to her. Just remembering what drugs to take and when can be a nuisance. The visits to physicians, physical therapists, alternative health practitioners, and other helpers increase with age as do the regimens suggested.

Obviously, the more time and energy expended on hassling over this and that, the less time and energy there is for relating and lovemaking.

The pain factor

Many acute and chronic diseases and injuries of matures involve physical pain. Sometimes pain is the whole problem. Consider one of the most common complaints of aging—back pain. Millions of older Americans suffer from it; millions are spent each year on a bewildering array of treatments, none of which appears to be successful with more than a small percentage of patients.

In other conditions, pain may be the first symptom of the problem, pain may come along later. If the condition itself does not cause pain, some of the treatments may. The most common symptom of another common affliction of aging, arthritis, is pain in the joints, especially pain with movement. And sex, you will recall, involves movement, often a considerable amount of it.

Surgery, far more common among matures than among the young, is also painful. In the hospital and at home, pain may continue for days, weeks, or months. It is truly amazing how often medical doctors understate the truth about this.

Some years ago I had surgery to correct an old high-school football injury to my shoulder. In the months following surgery, I went to a rehabilitation gym in the hospital to do corrective exercises, and there I met dozens of people similar to me, most with knee and shoulder problems. All of them, including me, complained that the doctors and surgeons had grossly understated the amount of postsurgical pain we would experience and for how long.

One usually doesn't want to be sexual when actually in pain, but the issue may go beyond this. One may be afraid to rock the boat. Say you're having a pretty good day, little or no pain, and the possibility of sex occurs to you. After all, it's been a while. But then fear sets in. What if having sex brings on the pain again? Do you really want to risk it? Is it worth it? Maybe it's better just to let things be. If you still feel okay tomorrow, perhaps you can try sex then. So sex can be put off repeatedly, until the absence of sex becomes an obstacle in itself, making sex in the future even more unlikely. One day you or your partner realizes that there's been no lovemaking in a year, or three years, or eight years, or even longer.

The main medical intervention for pain is pharmaceuticals. There's no doubt they alleviate pain. But almost without exception, they cause problems of their own, which we will address shortly.

Emotional factors

When we are young, most illnesses and injuries are taken in stride. Even if we have pneumonia or break a limb, long-term consequences and impact are usually not apparent. We will recover and continue on our way. That's as it should be because that is usually the case.

However, that is not so typical at midlife—and rarely in old age. We attach great meaning to our afflictions during these periods of life and usually with justification. It suddenly or gradually becomes manifest that we are not here forever and the end may be closer than we have anticipated. And if we have a certified killer such as high blood pressure, a heart ailment, or any one of the many cancers, we are suddenly face to face with the most difficult thing we humans have to confront, our own death. I don't mean to be maudlin, but as someone who almost died in the hospital a few years ago after losing over 35 pounds as a consequence of abdominal surgery and being unable to take any nutrition by mouth, I have a sense of what it's like. My point: looking at death, fearing death, even thinking about death—such things are not conducive to sexual interest or activity.

Another emotional factor to consider is the fear of doing harm to oneself or one's partner, of making the disease or injury worse. This is commonly seen in those who have had heart attacks. Despite all the good news from the medical community—that sexual activity is fine as soon as the patient is able to walk up a flight of stairs with relative ease—many heart disease sufferers, or their partners, still fear that sex will provoke another attack.

Then there is what sociologists call the patient role. It's a fact that when word gets around that we've had a heart attack or cancer or something equally appetizing, people treat us differently. They treat us as if we're ill. They ooze solicitousness and concern. While the behavior is meant to show caring, there's a downside. Their reactions

combined with our own, often make us feel less confident, less strong, less capable. These are not characteristics we associate with being sexual. And if our partner
shows too much concern, if she or he believes that we're
not strong enough for sex, those responses can affect us
negatively at a time when a positive sense of self is especially helpful.

The drug factor

Just as disease and disability are common among mature
citizens, so too are the prescription medicines designed to
combat them. The sheer number of drugs taken daily by
mature men and women is amazing. Just to give you a
point of reference, George Vaillant, Director of the
Harvard Study of Adult Development, reports that the
average 75-year-old takes three to seven different prescription medicines (2002, p. 155).

By now it is well known that a great many of the pharmaceuticals that help us also have serious side-effects,
especially sexual ones. The list is too long to go into here,
but the usual effects include decreased sexual interest,
inhibition of arousal and erections, and difficulty having
orgasms. These particular side-effects are quite common
among the best-known antidepressants such as Prozac,
Zoloft, and Paxil. In other words, many of the most high
tech and effective medicines make a mess of sex. If you
need a particular drug to live, you may have no choice
but to put up with its sexual consequences. But quite
often there's a similar medicine available with fewer
associated sexual consequences. The problem is that

physicians are unlikely to consider sexual side-effects unless the patient or the patient's partner make it clear that sex is important.

Several years ago I had a client in his early 50s who complained that he wasn't getting good erections. In the first interview, I asked my usual questions and got the usual answers, until we got to his health. He had high blood pressure for which he was taking the medicine, Aldomet, for about a year and a half—approximately the same length of time he had been experiencing erection problems. He was not aware that the drug was known to cause such problems. When I asked if he had ever told his doctor that a good sex life was important to him and his wife or if he and the doctor had ever discussed the potential sexual side effects of Aldomet, he said no. I suggested he and his wife go back to his physician and have both of these discussions. Two months later, I got a call from the man and he told me he followed my suggestion, and that the doctor had substituted a different blood pressure drug. Upon switching medications, his erections improved and he and his wife were grateful. This solution may sound too easy to be true, but that's really all it took, and there are numerous other examples like it.

Another problem with drugs, especially painkillers, is that they often cause drowsiness, which obviously doesn't make sex easier. And many of the painkillers can blitz you out altogether. It's hard to make love if you're barely conscious. Again, a talk with the doctor about the importance of sex can help a great deal.

Clearly, there are pros and cons to taking almost any medicine, including antidepressants and pain medicines. There is often a delicate balance between the benefits of the drug and the costs (which includes not only the financial costs but also the side-effects). You are indeed fortunate if you find a physician who listens to you and understands your health situation as well as what you value in life, and will help guide you to the best possible remedies for your current condition.

Good sex involves time, energy, and as well-functioning a body as is possible, plus a generally positive attitude and the ability to focus on the moment. Anything that interferes with these qualities—such as anything that takes away confidence, time, energy, or dims your ability to be present—will diminish sexual interest or functioning. I and many others are battling a number of less than sexually inspiring things in our lives. But do not give up. I can say with enthusiasm that my current sex life is one of the brightest aspects of my life.

Still, serious illnesses and their treatments, as well as disabilities all have negative effects on the sexual desire and functioning of people. Leslie Schover, one of our foremost authorities on the relationship between illness and sex, concludes:

 Men and women with a chronic illness are at heightened risk for having sexual problems. Chronic illness is a risk factor both because of the physiological changes from a disease or its treatment, and because of the psychological impact. Decreased frequencies of sex as well as high rates of sexual dysfunction have been documented in patients with cardiovascular disease, cancer, neurological disease, diabetes, end-stage renal disease, chronic obstructive pulmonary disease, and chronic pain. (Schover, 2000, p. 2)

My intent in this chapter was to provide honest and accurate information, but while it may be discouraging, there is also another side to the story. Edward Brecher, who conducted a survey for Consumer's Union nearly 20 years ago on sexuality among matures, reported:

We have found that impaired health has an adverse impact, but only a modest one, on sexual activity, sexual frequency, and sexual enjoyment. Both women and men continue to engage in sex, and to enjoy sex, despite health barriers, some of which to others might seem insuperable. Substantial proportions of respondents who have had a heart attack remain sexually active and continue to enjoy sex. The same is true of respondents who are taking antihypertensive medication, those with diabetes, and those who have had a hysterectomy, ovariectomy, mastectomy, or prostate surgery. (Brecher, 1984, pp. 406–407)

Medical problems and their treatments do present real obstacles to sexual desire, sexual functioning, and sexual pleasure. But these barriers are not total or absolute. Chapter 10, "What's Health Got To Do With It?", shows that those who value erotic expression with their partners can and do find ways to do it.

Other challenges

Poor health is not the only impediment to good sex in later life. The general busyness of adult life is certainly an oft-cited one. Where is one to get the time and energy to make love after a full day? Stress, disappointment, frustration, and failure at work are also among the culprits. And the major obstacle of all? Relationship woes. People who feel hostile toward, and distant from, their partners typically do not want to be intimate with them. A number of examples are described in Part 2, but for now, I offer the story of a couple with whom I worked several years ago in therapy. Their report illustrates how a number of factors—physical, and otherwise—can come together to make sex a rare and not very pleasing occurrence.

Within a two-year period all of the following happened to Harriet and Isaac, a couple in their late 40s. Isaac's son from his first marriage, then 24 years old, became an even greater problem than usual to his mother, with whom he lived. He quit college, refused to look for work, and just loafed around the house. He was apparently depressed, but his mother, a counselor herself, was unable to persuade him to seek help. Neither she nor Isaac were able to do anything with him. They felt too guilty to throw him out of the home, so they continued to support him, and his condition remained the same for several years. Isaac felt very bad about the situation and worried about it a lot, but his refusal to take any action made Harriet angry. She didn't want to hear about the situation anymore unless some action was going to be taken. This issue created serious distance between the couple.

During the same time, the restructuring going on in Isaac's company clearly indicated that although he would probably keep his job until retirement, there would be no chance for growth or promotion. Isaac didn't feel good about this either, but he was afraid to confront his employers or to leave the job to seek a better situation. Harriet lost some respect for him, and the situation became another source of tension between them.

Harriet then lost both a cousin and a close friend to heart disease. Since the disease ran in her family, she became increasingly depressed and experimented with a host of drugs, finally settling on Prozac, which did nothing for her already-faltering sex drive. Harriet's depression also brought Isaac down, and the couple's sense of mutual alienation continued to grow.

Adding to the mix, Harriet's health was slowly deteriorating. Her cholesterol, always high, was getting out of control and the medicine she was on seemed less and less effective at controlling it, which made her even more depressed, thus requiring stronger doses of Prozac. Likewise, her blood pressure was rising and she now required two drugs to help control it.

Given this information, which, believe it or not, is only part of the picture, it's probably understandable to the reader that they hardly related at all and couldn't recall the last time they had enjoyed or even had sex.

Isaac and Harriet's situation is not uncommon. As the issues in midlife accumulate, some medical, some not, relating well and making love may become a distant memory. The outcome of this situation may surprise you. It certainly surprised me. I spent over a year working with this couple in therapy and despite a very difficult journey for all three of us, things did improve. Harriet was able to cut down on her anti-depressant and then taper off it altogether. She and Isaac worked with his ex-wife and the three of them eventually threw the son out of the house. Most important, Harriet and Isaac started talking to one another again and having some pleasant and then some outright fun times. As these changes took place, affection became more common, and later on so did lovemaking. Although I wouldn't have predicted it at the beginning, this case turned out well. And although the account of Harriet and Isaac may sound extreme, I have seen many similar couples and a number of them were able to turn things around.

Starting over at midlife

I noted in the Introduction that there is always the possibility of a sexual second chance, that midlife offers the opportunity for many individuals and couples who are in a long relationship or a new one to start over again sexually. A common situation is when a man or woman ends up alone at age 45 or older due to divorce or the death of the partner.

Whether this is an obstacle or an opportunity depends on attitude. Some people do view it as a chance to do things over and better than the first time around. For others it is much more of a challenge because of their anxiety about the situation.

The causes of the anxiety are many. People feel bad enough about the mistakes they've made in the past and are afraid that they'll make them again or make new ones. Others worry about their attractiveness in the single's marketplace. Women, as previously noted, may worry about showing their aging body to a new partner. Will the cellulite, the wider hips, the less-than-firm buttocks, or the sagging breasts be a turnoff?

A woman in her late 50s laughingly recalled during my interview with her how she dealt with the situation after her divorce.

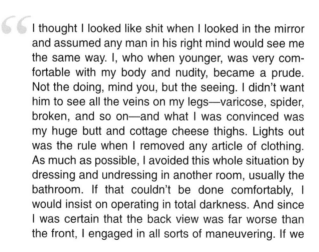

I thought I looked like shit when I looked in the mirror and assumed any man in his right mind would see me the same way. I, who when younger, was very comfortable with my body and nudity, became a prude. Not the doing, mind you, but the seeing. I didn't want him to see all the veins on my legs—varicose, spider, broken, and so on—and what I was convinced was my huge butt and cottage cheese thighs. Lights out was the rule when I removed any article of clothing. As much as possible, I avoided this whole situation by dressing and undressing in another room, usually the bathroom. If that couldn't be done comfortably, I would insist on operating in total darkness. And since I was certain that the back view was far worse than the front, I engaged in all sorts of maneuvering. If we

> were in bed and I had to go to the toilet, I always,
> always, backed away from him. He assured me to no
> end but it didn't help much. Walking in reverse in the
> dark became my m.o.

It's amazing what we do to ourselves in our never-ending quest for approval? Men also worry about acceptance and rejection. Will they be seen as successful enough, mature enough, strong enough?

The performance trap

For men, the possibilities of a sexual second chance at mid-life are often viewed positively, especially with a younger partner. But not always. There are plenty of men who are concerned about their ability to keep up with younger women. In the Introduction, I mentioned my own anxiety about being able to satisfy the sexy and expressive woman I met in 1996. She wasn't even that much younger than me, but she sure seemed to have a lot of energy and wasn't shy about expressing the importance of frequent and high-quality lovemaking. Until I got to know her better, I sometimes feared that the Bernie of 1966 might be a better physical match for her than the present one.

Gabe offers a good illustration of what some men go through. Forty-seven when I talked with him, he had been divorced three years and had dated only sporadically even though he desired the intimacy of a close relationship. When I asked what was preventing him from putting more effort into finding a mate, his reply indicated how much thought he had put into the subject.

> It comes down to a few things. One is that I'm scared of having another failed marriage. I'm still not sure what happened with Lillie. There were no affairs, no big deceptions, we rarely fought. Being together just got less and less interesting every year, to the point where we barely interacted at all in the five years before the breakup. I had my friends and activities, she had hers. We were civil and worked well together running the house, but it was more like a business arrangement than a love affair. In the last two years, I think we had sex only five or six times and I developed a problem getting hard. Anyway, I don't want another failure on my résumé and I'm not sure how to prevent it.
>
> Another thing is that because I really want a child and, to be honest, I'm more attracted to younger women anyway. I'm afraid that the women I'll be attracted to won't like me. Like they won't find me rich and successful enough. I do OK, but I'm not a mover and a shaker. An even bigger matter of concern is that I *will* be acceptable *until* we get into bed. Because of her age, she'll probably be used to guys who want sex every minute and can really give it to her. I'm not dead by any means, I desire and like sex, but not as often and as energetically as I did ten, fifteen years ago. There's also this damn erection problem. I started having trouble getting it up with Lillie the last few years we were together. Haven't had sex with anyone else since her, so I assume my performance is about the same. What is this gorgeous young thing going to think of me? Probably tell me to get lost. Shit! I've been thinking I need to talk to a doctor or to a shrink

about this, but for three years now, I've been too embarrassed to make the move.

Do men like Gabe ever get it together, find someone, and have good relationships and sex? Of course. But that usually requires finding a way out of the performance orientation, which means realizing that he's fine even though he's not a millionaire, even though he's had a failed marriage, and even though he has less than rock-hard erections. Especially in the sexual arena, men can only lose as they age if they persist in holding to a specific performance orientation. Progress becomes possible when such men realize that making love has more to do with a way of relating than with how well they perform and how hard they are. It's either this Realization— or munch Viagra all day long.

From my interviews, I learned that almost anything is possible. Women and men alike find new partners in midlife and many of them do create new relationships and sexual arrangements that are better than what they had before. It can happen with a younger partner, someone your own age, or someone older. Others, as already noted, improve their long-term relationships. The 40s, 50s, 60s, and 70s do not necessarily mean the end of anything. For some, midlife and beyond can present a new beginning or, if you prefer, a second chance, whether with a new or established partner. As long as one draws breath, there's an opportunity for growth and renewal. Obstacles and challenges abound as one grows older, but so do opportunities and possibilities.

Chapter 4

Advantages of Mature Sex

"The best tunes are played on the oldest fiddles."
                                                            —Anon.

Youngsters are often great sexual performers. Youthful
energy and stamina, almost continuous erections, hard
bodies, perky breasts, and gallons of testosterone and
estrogen gushing through the arteries define sex not only
in Hollywood but also in the minds of some aging baby
boomers who think they are washed up. Alfred Kinsey
was so impressed with the sexual capacity of the young
that 70 years ago he came to the conclusion that males
reach their sexual peak in their teens and females in their
30s, a notion that persists today in the minds of many.
This important issue deserves a little section of its own.

Genital performance vs good loving

What you need to know about Kinsey is that, like the Count on Sesame Street, he was basically a counter. The main thing he did was count and categorize; this was his main contribution and also his main failing. Unfortunately, many of us, including sex therapists, often forget this fact.

Some things, by their very nature, are easier to count than others. How does one go about quantifying feelings of passion, caring, closeness, relatedness, and satisfaction? It can be done, but it isn't easy. It is much easier to count things such as the frequency of masturbation and intercourse, the number of partners and orgasms. And that is what Kinsey did.

As already noted, Kinsey concluded from the count that males hit their sexual peak in the late teens because that's when they had the greatest number of orgasms per day, week, month, whatever. Women, on the other hand, didn't have their greatest frequency of orgasms until they were older. His conclusions have become part of our national consciousness. But is this how we want to evaluate sex, solely by the number of activities and orgasms per unit of time? Do we want genital performance to be our standard?

Let's look at teenage boys whose penises stand at attention with a moment's notice, but who are not known for their great interest in sensual play, or for their sexual knowledge or skill, sensitivity or caring, or their willingness or ability to relate well. I do not believe that most matures, given time for analysis and reflection, would choose this limited performance orientation in lovemaking for themselves or their partners. They want more, far more, than perfunctory sex. They want the whole package—foreplay, and intimacy, and intercourse, and afterglow, and ....

Sexual performance is by no means a road to good relationships or happiness. It's just what it says, performance. As we will discuss in more detail in Part 2, performance has virtually nothing to do with loving, satisfying, bonding, or mature lovemaking. One advantage of sex in the mature years is that those of us no longer young are more likely to choose to be great lovers instead of merely good performers.

Mature women and men are more in sync

As they age, women and men become much more like each other in many areas, including sex. Women can focus more on the purely physical aspects of sex and men can focus more on the emotional aspects. There is plenty of evidence that these transformations do indeed occur. Such mutual exchange can foster a more balanced and richer lovemaking.

Mature women
With all due respect to Kinsey, researchers these days do not believe that it's downhill for women after 30. There is convincing evidence that middle-age women continue to

grow and develop in the bedroom. Women in their 40s and 50s become more assertive, more self-confident, and very often more energetic sexually (Apter, 1995, p. 201). In my own interviews, women told me that at midlife they are more willing to initiate, be active, and to experiment. They say they are more likely to act on their own feelings of desire instead of simply reacting to their partner's desire, and that they are more prone to focus on the purely physical aspects of sex than when they were younger. One woman explained:

> I have become more experimental in my touching, kissing, sucking, feeling, and so on, which has been a turn on to the men I've been with. I also think I've achieved a level of confidence I didn't have in my younger years and I am much more attuned to my body. Sex has been the best ever in the last five years because of all these reasons.

I have also talked with a number of women who didn't have their first orgasm until their late 30s or their 40s and didn't feel they really got sex right until sometime in their 40s or 50s.

And of course one advantage menopause confers on women is freeing them from the possibility of conception and the need for contraception. From my interviews, I know this can be tremendously liberating in a sexual sense. Being a male, I wasn't aware of this issue until a few years ago when a woman friend set me straight. In talking about why she feels sexually freer than ever before, she said:

> Something that's made a big difference for me is knowing for certain that I can't get pregnant and also that I don't have to mess with birth control. This has been enormously liberating for me and also for other women I've talked to.

She reported that even though she was on the pill for many years, the possibility of getting pregnant, even though statistically almost nonexistent, was always in the back of her mind. "To some extent," she continued, "it always slowed me down. Now I'm totally free."

Mature men

As the years go by, most men slow down sexually. They are no longer in such a rush to get to orgasm. Those who were rapid ejaculators in their youth often find that the passage of the years has resolved the problem. They can take their time and enjoy the scenery. Men also become more focused on the emotional aspects of sex. They want, many for the first time ever, to really make love, to experience closeness and intimacy as much as orgasm. They may not be as good at performing as they used to be, but they are better lovers. A woman in her 50s describes these men:

> One thing that's definitely made sex better for me in recent years is being with older men, men who are not in a hurry to get sex over with and who relish foreplay.

A 55-year-old man who looks like a professional wrestler said this:

> " The guys I grew up with would never believe it was me talking, but the truth is that I now enjoy the leading-up-to part as much as the main event and the *cuddling* and *sleeping together* afterward is as important as the orgasm. I don't even reach orgasm every time we do it, but I enjoy it just the same. "

Familiarity can breed arousal

This is not so much about age as it is about being together for many years which, of course, is true for only some matures. For some men, this is the ultimate nightmare, having sex repeatedly for decades with the same partner. No matter how gorgeous and sexy she once was or still is, it's routine, boring, monotonous, and not at all a thrill. What these men want is not simply sex, but variety.

No doubt this is the attitude of some men. But not all. There are men, and women as well, who are turned on by having the same partner year after year, decade after decade. I think it is fitting that my favorite story about these people comes from a man:

> " I don't see what the big deal is about new partners and the boredom so many people report about having sex with the same person for many years. In sex as in so many other areas of my life, I prefer familiarity— knowing and being known—to newness, strangeness, and unpredictability. I like that my wife's body and behavior in sex is known to me, it's predictable. That makes me comfortable and enhances my arousal. Being with someone new would make me

anxious and she'd probably be anxious as well. What's so great about that?

Last year when we were shopping for a new car, several owners and reviewers praised the Toyota Camry to the hilt yet complained that it was boring. I, on the other hand, would be bragging, as I did about the old Camry we were wanting to replace. I don't want adventure or excitement from my car. When I turn the key, I want it to start. When I press the brake, I want it to stop. I don't want to hear strange noises, don't want to see smoke coming out of the engine or the rear end. Spare me such drama. I want a car I can depend on. I feel the same about my partner and sex with her. Spare me the surprises. I gladly leave them for my single friends.

Practice makes better

Practice may not make perfect, but it certainly does lead to improvement. I like what Robert Parker, the author of the best-selling Spencer detective novels, puts in the mouth of his favorite private investigator regarding this subject in his recent work: "Susan and I had been making love with one another for quite a number of years now, and had gotten quite expert" (Robert B Parker, 2002, p. 290).

Couples who have been together many years often say that lots of practice is what makes sex so good for them. They have accumulated knowledge—not in their heads but in their bones—about what it takes to satisfy themselves and their partners. It's not only knowledge but also the trust and comfort with one another that evolves over the years.

I think this 54-year-old man speaks for many matures:

> Sex is great because we know each other well. We know each other's hot buttons and also trouble spots. When one is not in the mood, the other knows enough not to press on, they back off. It's a twosome as opposed to two different entities, each concerned only with their own gratification. Pleasing my partner is a total turn-on. A great relationship is critical to good sex, and vice versa.

Control of emotion improves with age

Apparently, mellowness increases with age and getting along with others becomes easier. Many older couples express less negative emotion and demonstrate more affection than younger couples. Even the discussion and resolution of conflict can be less emotionally negative and more affectionate. One of the first to mention this was the psychoanalyst Erik Erikson. Fifty years ago he noted that:

> Those in late midlife describe both themselves and their aged contemporaries as more tolerant, more patient, more open-minded, more understanding, more compassionate and less critical than they were in their younger years (quoted in Vaillant, 2002, p. 144).

Most of the Lovers reported they had mellowed over the years, and become more mature, wiser, more accepting, better able not to sweat the small things and not to take things personally. Why are these characteristics important to us? These changes make it easier to establish and maintain the kind of relationship necessary to support a passionate sexuality. After all, criticism, defensiveness, inflexibility, and arguments usually do not put one in the mood for lively sex.

Mature lovers appreciate what they have

In youth there's a tendency to take things for granted, including one's love relationships. Midlife, however, gives us all a chance to reappraise our values and priorities. Some women and men—though not all—come to realize just how precious their sweetheart is, whether in a new relationship or one of many years' duration. This acknowledgement offers everyone who is interested the opportunity for a second chance, a new direction. For a great many couples, this means a greater emphasis on closeness, affection, and sex. Many people realize for the first time how precious being in love and making love are, and are less likely to take love and sex for granted. This greater appreciation for deeper connection is in part why matures are more willing to make time for togetherness.

Mature lovers have more time for intimacy

One consequence of the midlife reappraisal and repriori-
tizing is the willingness often seen in those over 50 and 60
to make more time for intimacy. While there are exceptions, of course, I was impressed by how many of the
Lovers interviewed mentioned this change. They are
willing and happy to set aside whole mornings or after-
noons for togetherness and sometimes whole days and
even weeks. A number of the Lovers mentioned taking
frequent trips, "just the two of them." For the majority of
these people the children are gone, so no more concerns
about being overheard or being walked in on.

Sex therapists and couple counselors are constantly
recommending that clients take time for togetherness and
lovemaking. But it's usually a tough sell because the
clients are raising children, making their mark on the
world, trying to make ends meet financially, and generally running around like there is no tomorrow. They
don't have time for anything. But the over-50 group, and
especially the over-60 group, is much more willing to
make time to appreciate today. Not only are they willing
to set aside more time in general, but also per encounter.

A number of men and women told me that when
younger, their sexual interactions usually took 15 or
20 minutes. Now, it's more like an hour or even longer. I
like the way this man put it: "When I was younger and
wanted sex, I was interested in a 20-minute deal. Now
when I want sex, I want to luxuriate in it, I want a

two-hour interaction." And his wife absolutely loves the change.

Given the amount of time older people spend in each lovemaking session, it's quite possible they spend more time having sex than people in their 20s, who may have more sessions but spend much less time on each one. (See more on this point in Chapter 8 "Intention".)

Sex is sex

I know there are lots of people who can't imagine mature sex having some advantages over youthful sex. I am amazed at how often I hear the following question from young people: But what do they do? They seem to think that if senior sex exists at all, it must be kind of strange and cumbersome, perhaps with both partners keeping their eyes closed the whole time so they won't have to look at the ugliness of their own or their partner's body and with lots of preparation and adjustments as they put aside their medicines and canes or walkers, or maneuver their wheelchairs into just the right positions. Let me state what should be obvious: *Sex is sex, young or old.*

Take a couple in their 20s. They will probably start with holding and kissing, proceed to touch each other on many parts of the body, there may be special attention paid to the woman's breasts with touching, licking, and sucking; there will almost certainly be hand stimulation of the genitals and maybe oral stimulation as well, and then there will probably be intercourse. There are other things as well. The lovers may have their eyes closed or they may open them and look at one another; they may undress one another or just themselves; they may have the lights on or blinds open, or they may be in the dark; they may talk during sex or not; they may talk dirty or share fantasies, or not; they may take their time about what they are doing or make quick work of it.

All of these options are available to everyone, regardless of age, national origin, religion, or any other attribute. Since sex as I have defined it has something to do with nakedness and genitals, it may not be easy for everyone to deal with. Some may not like to think of their mothers or fathers or grandparents being nude doing things with each other's genitals, but their dislike or disgust does not change the facts. There are people at every age who have great sex. And it may be fewer in their 20s and 30s than you might imagine—and more in their 50s and beyond. As we will see in Part 2, it takes many years to get sex right.

Sex problems are sex problems

You may still be skeptical if you've internalized the Hollywood version of reality. You may think that you have to be young and beautiful to have great sex. You may romanticize your youth, forgetting the sexual traumas and feelings of inadequacy. Take it from me as a sex therapist: every age group has problems with sex and in the main they overlap. So not only do young and old engage in the same behaviors, they also experience and are annoyed by the same problems. Common at all ages are desire discrepancies (one partner wanting more sex than the other), difficulties getting aroused, problems getting and keeping erections, the man not lasting long enough before ejaculating, the woman not being able to orgasm, pain with intercourse (usually for the woman), and difficulties in sexual communication or finding time for sex.

What's true about sexual problems is also true about finding a partner and getting into a relationship. When older people lose a partner to death or divorce and start to look for a new partner, they seem strikingly similar to people half their age looking for a partner. Concerns about one's attractiveness, desirability, and sex appeal are common at all ages. Many single older women and men have told me that their feelings and concerns are very similar to when they were teenagers or in their 20s.

Even physical problems are not necessarily age-specific. Many seniors, because of various health problems and medical conditions, have to make modifications in how they have sex, but they're not the only ones. I'll use myself as an example. When I was 33 years old, I ruptured a disk in my lower back. I had virtually every treatment known and nothing helped for over a year. Any bending, twisting, or almost any movement of my pelvis generated serious pain in my back and all the way down one leg. Shortly after my injury, I became involved with a woman. Because of my disk, there were many things I could not do. The only intercourse position I could manage with relative comfort was with her on top because that way she did all the work and I didn't have to move my pelvis much. So, for almost a year, that's the only way we had intercourse. And it wasn't only intercourse that required accommodation. No matter what kind of caressing and stimulating we did, I always had to be very careful what position I assumed and, despite being careful, I often experienced pain and sometimes had to stop what we were doing, or at least take a break.

Many people in their 20s and 30s break limbs, sprain muscles, and otherwise hurt themselves in sports and accidents. Although the effects of these injuries are usually time-limited, they nonetheless usually require sexual adjustments.

And let's not forget pregnancy and child rearing. Many a couple has found that especially in the third trimester of pregnancy, different intercourse positions and different practices have to be adopted. Immediately after childbirth, especially if the woman is breast-feeding, she is often not able or inclined to be sexual. For many couples, the years of having young children in the house also require dramatic changes in their sexual patterns. Even assuming the partners have enough time and energy to want sex, long, leisurely encounters may be impossible. Quickies, dictated by when the baby goes down for a nap, may be the necessary compromise. Even when the children are older, many parents still feel the need to adjust: they may make love only when the children are out of the house, or only after they're asleep, and they may also feel the need to stifle their natural exclamations of pleasure and delight.

Okay, so younger people have obstacles too, but it's matures we are talking about in this book. Let's go on.

Differences in senior sex

The partner gap

After age 50, there are not enough men for the number of available women. The men start dying off in greater numbers than the women do at around 50, and this trend continues as both groups get older. In one study, half the women ranging in age from 60 to 74 and 80 percent of the women 75 and older had no sex partner. This is a sad situation and I don't know of any solutions for it. There have been suggestions for years that older women should seek out younger men or other women. These ideas may have a certain logic to them, the fact is that the vast majority of older women do not act on them. As a result, the partner gap remains.

Less acrobatic sex

A number of those over 50 to whom I talked mentioned that because of medical conditions, physical discomfort, or lack of energy, sex is less acrobatic these days than before. You can either wallow in your lack of energy or you can adjust to a different but still pleasurable sex life. One woman I interviewed who's still having great sex with her husband of 60 years summed it up this way: "It's less wild, but not less good." The couple that once had sex in the back seat of the car, on the kitchen counter, the living room coffee table, or standing up in the shower, may now find it's most convenient and comfortable and doable to have sex in their bed. The couple that used to have a lot of fast and furious encounters may now find they prefer more leisurely lovemaking. These accommodations do not necessarily mean that the sex is less passionate, less pleasurable, less loving, or less fulfilling.

I hope it's clear that less acrobatic in the paragraph above means that and only that. Most matures are no longer capable of contorting their bodies the way they could when younger. Their arthritis or some other condition will no longer allow it, or no longer allow it in a pain-free manner. But this does not mean necessarily mean that matures are less experimental and free in their activities. I have numerous reports of women and men trying out new positions, new places, and new practices after age 50 or 60. Some couples didn't get around to checking out oral sex until their fifth or sixth decade. Some waited as long to try sex on the air mattress or the rocking chair.

I end this chapter by reiterating: Women and men of all ages are capable of feeling sexual and behaving erotically with themselves or their partners. Further, there are advantages to being older and wiser. Remember the saying: "Youth is wasted on the young." Well, don't waste maturity. Sagging breasts, soft penises, paunches, gray hair and baldness, and wrinkles and cellulite have as much a right to good sex as young hard bodies and can participate in it just as passionately. I wonder how many more years it will take before Hollywood figures this out.

Part 2

Chapter 5

The Non-lovers

Before getting to the Lovers, I thought it would be instructive to look at some examples of not so terrific sex, the kind of eroticism experienced by most people most of the time, what I think of as ordinary sex. Accordingly, I put the interview transcripts of the participants who hadn't rated their sex as very good or excellent in a pile and randomly pulled out seven of them. I was pleased when I read the chosen transcripts because they cover a lot of ground, from reasonably good sex to no partner sex to no partner and no sex. I think these cases fairly represent what goes on in a lot of homes in America. According to the best surveys available, the amount of sex Americans engage in has been seriously exaggerated in the popular media—and in our minds. These women and men, as much as anyone else, are part of the picture of sex in America.

Jesse and Barb

Fifty-five years old at the time of the interview, Jesse has been married to Barb for over 30 years. They have raised two children who are now on their own. Both husband and wife are in good health and neither is taking any prescribed medicines. Although Jesse characterizes the quality of his marriage and his sex life as "middling to good", he also gives a number of indications that there are significant problems in both areas.

Jesse describes himself as a "distant" person, to whom closeness does not come easily. Although he thinks he's become less selfish over the years, more able to understand his wife's point of view, and more willing to consider her needs in sex as well as his own, he's still distant in a number of ways.

He's not much of a talker, and Barb has her own problems with communication. Four times during the course of the marriage Jesse felt he wasn't getting the attention he wanted from Barb. Rather than discuss the situation with her and try to rectify it, he sought solace in an affair. When we got into detail about the timing of the affairs, it was clear in each instance that his wife was preoccupied, either with a new child or a new job, and was therefore not as available to cook dinner for him, keep him company when running errands, or hear about problems at his job. Regarding the quality of the affairs, he reported the sex as "OK" and that while at first it was good to have someone totally attentive to him for the short amount of time they were together, the appeal soon paled, and he realized it wasn't worth it, and so he terminated the affair.

Just as he couldn't tell his wife about wanting more attention, he can't tell her when he wants sex or specifically what he wants in bed. "My communication about when I want sex is terrible," he acknowledges and then adds: "I think we are still shy with each other, even after all these years. I don't know why, but it's just so difficult for me to come right out and say what I want. Barb isn't much better."

In addition, there is also a huge affectional discrepancy. Barb is a toucher and Jesse isn't. As he says, "Affectionate touching has never played a role in my life. We rarely touch in public; that's my doing. She would absolutely like more touching. She likes hugging and cuddling and hand holding and all those things. They just don't fit for me. In fact, they're foreign to me."

Barb would like sex more often than the once or so a month they have it, but Jesse is content with what they have. He thinks that lack of time is the main reason for not having more sex and suggests he'd have to win the lottery to have enough money to take the time to engage in more frequent sex. He also mentions that having his ill father living with them for the last two years may be a factor. "After all, dad is demanding and requires a lot of looking after." But when he considers this more deeply, he modifies his perspective: "I don't really think it's time or my father. We could make the time if we wanted to, we certainly waste a lot of it on stupid things like hours of television watching, and my father's been here long enough that I think we have that situation pretty well worked out. If I could just get over my thing of being such a distant person, we'd probably have more sex and I'd be happier with myself and she would be happier with me."

Now, Jesse has matured over the years and has become a better lover. Although his desire has decreased with the passing years and it takes longer to get aroused, he's become more attentive to his partner. "Over time," he reports, "I've become more willing to do something for her before I orgasm. We work together on it."

Working together, however, does not include giving oral sex to Barb. Jesse knows she would like it—she's expressed her wishes about it several times, although never too directly or firmly—but, as Jesse puts it, "I don't know why, but I just can't do it. I'd tried once or twice early on and I couldn't go on. Maybe I think it's dirty or something."

His orgasm is what's most important to him and he has one virtually every time. Jesse says he feels closer to his wife during sex, "It does bring us together." When I ask him specifically about Barb's enjoyment and orgasm, he replies that he thinks she also has orgasms and is satisfied, but he's not certain. Since they don't talk about sex at all, it's difficult to know for sure, but he infers it from the common refrain they sing after lovemaking. "Generally, I think that sex with us is pretty standard everyday stuff. Well, every month stuff. When we have sex we say, 'God, we ought to do this more often.' So I think we're both enjoying it. But then another three or four weeks pass and we go, 'Didn't we say we were going to do this more often?' How that happens I don't know."

I have the sense in talking with Jesse that he might be open to change, to being less distant and more intimate, if some outside leverage were applied. In other words, if Barb insisted on couples therapy, I think he would be willing. After all, he indicated several times that he knows his distance and lack of touching are serious problems. Unfortunately, he can't seem to take the first step on his own. And given that Barb isn't very assertive either, it's highly unlikely there will be any change in this marriage.

The fear of closeness exemplified by Jesse is commonly associated with not desiring or having frequent sex and also with an unwillingness to do anything to improve its quality (in this case, oral sex for his wife). In this couple we also see something very common in couples whose sex lives are less than sparkling— serious difficulties talking about sexual and intimacy issues.

Also worthy of mention are Jesse's affairs, the stimulus for which, he claims, was not getting as much of Barb's attention as he wanted. I would assume that given her general attitude (strong commitment to their marriage as well as wanting more touching and more sex), this situation could have been rectified easily had he brought it up. Instead of doing this, however, he sought attention elsewhere. This was not the best way to deal with the perceived problem, as he himself concedes. Seeking solutions in all the wrong places is common among the non-Lovers I interviewed. Lovers are far better at finding appropriate fixes for the problem at hand.

Tina and Bob

While working on this book, I've been asked many times if it's possible to have a great marriage and a poor sex life. Tina's story goes a long way to answering that question. Her 40-year marriage is the envy of all who know her. She and Bob are best friends, spend lots of time together, and are very respectful, caring, and supportive. Anger is a bit of a problem for them—they both suppress it and some things never get resolved or even discussed. They are both careful not to say or do things that will anger the other. This way of dealing with differences and anger is not for everyone, but all in all it works for them and they have a strong union.

Sex, however, is another story altogether. It was "awful" when they first got together and has improved only slightly over the years. They were both virgins and were unable to help each other. "In this case," she says, "it was the blind *not* leading the blind. Neither of us took the lead." As a result, Tina was anorgasmic for over 15 years.

A huge problem is that there was never much physical chemistry between them. Their primary attraction was in other areas. They assumed they would develop a stronger sexual bond over time, but it didn't happen. Bob doesn't do things in ways that arouse Tina, and she has been unwilling/unable to teach him what she likes. One reason for this failure is the lack of chemistry. Another is their inability to talk about sex, either during or outside of it. Add the fact that Bob has had erection problems since the beginning, which were not helped by a course of sex therapy or, more recently, Viagra. My guess is that the lack of chemistry is a major contributor to this dysfunction. In turn, the erection difficulty is just another obstacle for them sexually.

Tina and Bob have sex maybe once a month these days. Both of their desires have decreased significantly in recent years. Tina attributes her decreased desire to the effects of menopause, her declining health, and the fact that she doesn't enjoy sex with Bob that much. She is regularly orgasmic but her main pleasure in lovemaking is satisfying Bob. Her explanation: "Even though the passion is lacking, he's a good man and I love him. If I can do something to make him happy, even for a few minutes, of course I'll do it." Despite the regular orgasms on both sides, the lack of chemistry and passion is an enduring problem. Over the years Tina had a number of brief affairs where the sex and communication about sex were much better, but she discontinued this habit some time ago because she feared the effect on the marriage and also, she explains, because, "Affairs are hard work and it just wasn't worth the effort."

Tina says she regrets that, "We didn't spend more time at the beginning learning about each other's sexuality. We're both smart people, I think we could have done much better." Now, with their sexual patterns hardened by decades of repetition, and with her desire having decreased sharply, she sees no hope for change.

Don't assume that Tina and Bob are unhappy. They aren't. Their strong marriage sustains them and they spend more time than most couples having fun playing golf and tennis, visiting children and grandchildren, and traveling to exotic places. Their lot in life, they will tell you, is a good one and they feel fortunate in having each other. And then, after a moment of silence, there's the whispered, "If only sex were better, we'd have it all."

Here again, as with Jesse and Barb, we see an inability to communicate about sex. For Tina and Bob, the results were devastating. Had they been able to talk at the beginning, there would have at least been a chance that they could have headed in a more positive erotic direction, even with the lack of chemistry. In fact, the absence of compelling sexual attraction made talking all the more necessary—but probably all the more difficult as well.

Speaking of which, this story offers a good lesson in what to look for in a partner and relationship. Although most couples have more than enough sexual attraction at the start, some couples do not. It is something altogether different that brings them together—shared values, common hobbies, similar professional interests, intellectual or emotional appeal, or some other nonsexual component. This is fine for people to whom sexual expression is not a high priority. But if it is, this may not be a good setup. I have seen many clients like Tina and Bob who, five, ten, or fifteen years after hooking up realize that the sexual passion they missed at the beginning and assumed would develop over time did not do so. Sexual chemistry does not usually develop as the years go by. It's not that it's impossible to generate some excitement later on, but it can be arduous work without any guarantee of success.

Tina's affairs were as ineffective as Jesse's in solving the problems. Tina learned what so many others have also learned: affairs are risky and are also very hard work. They are not easy to start or maintain, and the sneaking around, making tactical arrangements, and constructing and remembering the stories to cover the deceit all requires time and energy.

So while an excellent relationship is an important ingredient for great sex over the long term, it is not, as Bob and Tina demonstrate, sufficient in itself.

Stan and Faith

Given that he's 76 years old, Stan is in remarkably good health. He has no major illnesses or conditions and takes no pills except for vitamins. He was happily married for 33 years until his wife died of cancer. His second marriage, to Faith, is now in its fifth year, and it is not a happy union. The main problems, he says, are that Faith is not flexible, is extremely critical, and does not tolerate differences of opinion; whenever they disagree on something, no matter what the topic, she withdraws.

Stan and Faith rarely have sex now because she's so upset about his quick ejaculations (Stan is one of the exceptions to the rule that men's quick ejaculations tend to get better as they get older). "Although I miss sex," he reports, "I don't look forward to being with her. I know she'll be unhappy with something and I'll feel incompetent. It's gotten so we hardly even hold hands, let alone make love." Faith can only orgasm through prolonged intercourse. She's never masturbated, won't hear of it, and doesn't want prolonged oral or manual stimulation. He suggested a vibrator, but she got upset and said she didn't want to hear about it again. She doesn't know how to orgasm with hand or mouth stimulation and has no interest in finding out how. "She's pretty closed off to different ways. My first wife was different. I was always a little quick on the trigger but she made do. If she wanted to have longer intercourse, she'd get on top because she knew I could hold off longer that way. It did last longer with her on top. She'd have her orgasm, I'd have mine, and we were happy. My current wife doesn't want to have to think about different things or do things differently. She likes me on top or from the back, where I don't have much lasting power. I asked her to get on top and she did once or twice but decided she doesn't like it that way, and that was that."

Stan has tried several different medications in the last three years to help him last longer, small doses of antidepressant drugs that for many men have the side effect of delaying orgasm. Unfortunately, they also caused him erection difficulties, so he stopped taking them.

Stan is not a happy man. He would like to recapture some of the bliss he felt in and out of bed with his first wife, but he has no idea of how to go about it. He tried talking to Faith about his feelings, but each time she reacted with stony silence. When he suggested that the two of them go for marital or sexual counseling, she became angry and didn't speak to him for a week. Although divorce is anathema to him, he said at the end of the interview that he has started to consider the possibility. We will run into Stan again because he and his first wife were Lovers. They had a satisfying sex life for over three decades and that, combined with Stan's current situation, has a crucial lesson to teach us about the importance of having the right partner if you want a good sex life.

In this case, we see the complete absence of one of the essential attributes of a superior sex life—an effective problem-solving mode that necessarily includes the ability to talk openly about the issues and flexibility about possible solutions. In the following chapters, we will see how the presence of these two factors can lead to forging positive solutions.

Angie and Richard

Although Angie is too young to be part of my sample (she was 44 when interviewed), her husband of five years is almost 50. This is a second marriage for both. They both describe the marriage as good but needing more work. Making time to be together away from their two children (one each from their first marriages) is an ongoing problem. Between work, children, and chores, they don't find much quality time to be together. When they are alone together, they tend to be "wiped out", as Angie put it, and half asleep. Nonetheless, they are able to talk about most things and work out conflicts.

Although they both say sex is good, they also say it needs help. Given the trouble they have finding time to be together, it's not surprising they also have trouble finding time to make love and these are the main complaints they both have—not enough time, not enough sex and, as we shall soon see, their different styles of lovemaking. They went from sex every day, sometimes more than once, in the first six months of their relationship, to barely once a week. Although it seems that Richard has a higher sex drive than Angie, neither is happy with the frequency they now have.

Angie says this about the sex they have: "I love making love with Richard. It's exciting, it really is making love, and it makes us feel closer for days afterward. At least when it's good. It's not always good, though, because our styles are somewhat different. I like there to be 'preforeplay,' some indication before sex actually begins that that's what we're going to do, so I can get in the mood. Sometimes when Richard initiates, it strikes me as odd. I mean, where did this come from? There have been no sexual touches or words for hours or days and suddenly he wants to make love. Or at least it seems sudden to me. I'd like sexual touching and words to be a more regular part of our lives."

Angie continues: "We touch a lot. We're big cuddlers and hand-holders. But the touch I get from him is the affectionate kind— loving, sensitive, and caring to be sure—but not erotic. There's no sense or hint of any erotic impulse behind it. That's what I want."

Richard's side: "The sex we have is terrific, but there can be problems when I initiate. Angie is sometimes surprised by it. She needs a foreplay to foreplay to get ready. I'm not like that. Almost anything can make me feel sexual and want to have sex. But she needs more time to get her head in the right space. I've heard her say this for years, but somehow it's hard for me to keep it in mind. Sometimes I'll go for weeks without initiating because it's just easier to wait for her to do it; then I know she's in the mood and I don't have to worry about getting into a hassle about it later. That's not a complete solution, however, because she likes me to initiate, and I want to be able to get sex when I want it and not just have to wait for her to make an advance. I know I need to do more with the sexual touching and words she wants. Oh Lord, why does this have to be so complicated!"

This problem has been brought up countless times by Angie, but the conversations tend not to be helpful. According to both of them, Richard usually listens silently, promises to do better, and nothing changes.

There's another issue that mars sex between Angie and Richard. As Richard puts it, "Sometimes Angie almost makes me crazy. She can be so specific and exacting, in the kind of stimulation she wants that I don't feel I can do it. It's like we're talking about hundredths of an inch to the left or right, or just this amount of pressure, or this fast or slow in such small increments I'm not sure they're measurable. I want to make her happy, I want to give her what she wants, but at times I just get anxious and really screw it up." Angie is aware of Richard's anxiety about her guidance, but this is an issue they can't talk productively about and it's remained at pretty much the same level since they were first together.

Because Angie and Richard have tried without success for years to make changes in their sexual relationship, I think they could benefit from counseling. There simply doesn't seem to be an alternative because their own discussions about sex go nowhere. I hope they decide to get this help. The kinds of problems they are having—lack of time, not as much sex as either wants, and differing sexual styles—can usually be resolved relatively easily when there is love, trust, and commitment.

Ken

Ken, 48, was highly stressed when I talked with him. His life in the last few years had been, as he characterized it, "a series of shocks that almost did me in." He had not yet fully come to terms with the fact that Miriam, his wife of 17 years, left him three years earlier. Although he knew the marriage had many problems, he was shocked when Miriam told him she had found someone else and was leaving.

Their relationship had been, according to him, very close, comforting, and exciting the first few years. With the benefit of hindsight, he now realized that there was no big event that broke it apart but rather a gradual, almost unnoticeable erosion. They started spending less time together, doing fewer things to please each other, having less physical affection and sex. He spent more and more time at work and on his "hobby", all sorts of woodworking projects. At the same time, Miriam spent more time with her friends and at her job.

A few years before the end, they both seemed to realize what was going on, and while the atmosphere at home became more gloomy and discouraging, neither took any heroic steps to save the marriage. One reason, Ken believes, is the absence of children; had they had children, he thinks, he would have tried to do something to avert a split.

Ken was deeply affected when Miriam asked for a divorce. Even though he did not want the marriage as it was—by now he more fully appreciated what an empty shell it had become—in his dictionary divorce was synonymous with failure. Given the fact of the divorce, it was difficult to feel good about himself. This self-doubt was reinforced by another disturbing fact: Miriam left him for a woman. Nothing in his background had prepared Ken for such a situation, and he was both bewildered and depressed by it.

Shortly after they separated, Ken received another shock: he was diagnosed with prostate cancer. Although it had been caught early and the prognosis was therefore quite favorable, it was not an easy situation to deal with, especially alone. Miriam, now living on her own and deeply ensconsed in her new relationship, offered what emotional support and physical assistance she could, as did her girlfriend, much to Ken's amazement, but this was a far cry from what he needed.

Ken carefully researched the available treatment options and wasn't happy with any of them. This is understandable given that each is known to cause sexual problems (erection and orgasm difficulties) and incontinence for a significant number of patients. He was particularly concerned about the erection issue. Although sex with Miriam had been frequent and "pretty damn good" at the start of their relationship, over the years he found that there were times he couldn't get or keep his erection. He interpreted this to mean that he was sexually inadequate. The prospect of an operation for prostate cancer was all he needed, a treatment that would further blunt his ability to be a good lover with a new partner.

Finally, Ken elected to have a nerve-sparing radical prostatectomy; in English, this means complete removal of the prostate to ensure that all the malignancy is destroyed while at the same time avoiding damage to the nerves that control erection. The surgeon and Ken's physician thought the surgery went well. In the more than two years since the operation, all signs suggest that the cancer has been completely removed and Ken's health is excellent.

Although Ken is relieved by this news, he is still quite troubled. Notwithstanding the surgeon's claim that the procedure spared the nerves, Ken's erections by himself are, by his observations, much more difficult to come by than before and not as rigid. Additionally, a new problem had surfaced: getting to orgasm had become an arduous task requiring more time and stimulation than ever before. He described his situation: "I feel like one of these women you hear about, who needs 12 hours of foreplay and endless clitoral stimulation to achieve orgasm. That's me now. In the past, if I was in a hurry I could get off in probably less than a minute. Since the operation, I don't think I've once had an orgasm in less than 30 minutes, and that's with the accompaniment of sex magazines and videos, things I didn't need at all before; now I can't seem to do anything without them."

Although it is likely that the surgery has damaged his erectile capability, Ken is fortunate that it did not lead to urinary incontinence. But this doesn't stop him from worrying about the possibility. Despite the reassurances of the surgeon and his own physician, he frets that he might start dripping or even gushing urine and be forced to wear an adult diaper. Such concerns, of course, don't do much to raise his confidence in his sexual abilities.

In the year before our interview, Ken briefly dated two women. Without giving any thought to the matter or consciously seeking

out a particular type of woman, it turned out that both were considerably younger than he was. Shana was strikingly beautiful
and eighteen years his junior. His fears surfaced immediately.
Could he keep up with such a young and energetic woman, sexually and otherwise? What did she want and expect in a man?

It didn't take long for his worst fears to be confirmed. Despite his
attraction to her, Shana soon proved to be everything Ken
feared. She was quite aggressive in all ways, always pushing
for what she wanted. He recounted: "God, I felt surrounded and
embattled. She had a never-ending list of things she wanted to
do. As soon as I agreed to one, she'd bring up another. The idea
of staying at her place or mine for the evening, just being
together, never seemed to be OK with her. We always were on
the go. And sexually, you wouldn't believe it. She had her
tongue in my mouth and her hand on my crotch on the first date!
I knew women had changed in the 20 years I'd been with
Miriam, but I didn't realize how far they had gone. Shana was as
forward as any man I ever heard of. That made me extremely
nervous and that led to a constant inability to function with her.
I was literally trembling, and not from passion. I didn't get hard
or lost the hard-on as soon as there was any attempt to enter
her. The whole time we were together, three months as I recall,
only two or three times did we have intercourse that lasted more
than a few seconds. She must have had hundreds of orgasms
with my hand and mouth, but I didn't get off once. I don't know
how much of this was due to anxiety, certainly some of it, and
how much to the surgery. But whatever it was, I could sure live
without it."

Ken stopped seeing Shana because being with her made him
feel anxious and like a failure. "I was lonely without her," he

recounts, "but I felt so much better alone than when I was with her. At least I didn't feel like a loser all the time."

Apparently, Ken was attractive to women and it didn't take him long to find another woman. But his experiences with her were similar to the ones with Shana, and in less than two months he stopped seeing the second woman. Although Ken acknowledges he has some good points—good health, good looks, a good job and income, and a great sense of humor (which was evident during our interview in spite of the hard times he was going through)—he strongly believes he is profoundly flawed as a romantic/sexual partner. He did not blame Shana. "Despite my abysmal sexual performance," he said, "she cared for me and really wanted to make the relationship work. Several times she suggested we go to therapy to straighten out the sexual problems, but I just couldn't handle that at the time." She even gave him a copy of my book, *The New Male Sexuality*. Although he didn't read it at the time, he recognized my name in an ad I had placed to attract interviewees and that was largely why he agreed to talk with me.

Looking back at his two short dating experiences, he says: "I'm still not sure it was the best decision to abruptly stop seeing them, but being with them was more than I could take. Even without the sex problems, they were just too energetic and aggressive for me. I don't have that much energy anymore. Sometimes I just want to zone out in front of the TV, or be quiet and read or work on my projects. I don't always feel up to talking nonstop for hours or running around town doing this and that. I felt like a failure much of the time."

Except in sex, he continues, "Where I felt like a failure *all* the time. Maybe it was a mistake being with someone so much younger. If I try again, I want a woman closer to my age, but I still want her to look good, not like some of these women in their 40s who look like old hags. With my luck, I'll probably find someone my age who has a libido the size of Canada."

Ken seems depressed and discouraged about his future during the interview. Despite frequent assurances from his doctor that there's no evidence of the tumor recurring or having mestasticized, he worries about his health. After all, the malignancy could return. Even if it doesn't, he has erection and orgasm difficulties, and could possibly end up not being able to fully control his bladder.

At one point during our interview, he laughed and said the following: "Can you imagine my personal ad on the Net? 'Middle-age man with only moderate amount of energy and passion, not able to boogie all night as he did in youth. Prostate cancer could recur without notice, so longevity is problematic. Anxious about dating after a failed marriage of 20 years duration. Possessed of several sexual dysfunctions, including difficulty keeping erections and inability to have orgasms without prolonged and harsh stimulation. Might have to wear diapers in the future. Would like to meet a lovely and together almost middle-age woman interested in romance.' Bet I'd have a lot of takers, don't you!"

Nonetheless, Ken acknowledges that he doesn't feel complete without a partner and would like someday to get married again. "I just hoped I learned enough from the relationship with Miriam not to make the same mistakes again. I didn't realize how easily and quietly a relationship can slip away. Next time, I can't afford to take it for granted. I guess you have to keep working at it to keep it alive and growing. I just hope I can make the changes I need and that I find someone who'll accept me." Just before concluding our interview, Ken says he hopes I am willing to answer a few questions for him. When I say I will do my best, he asks if it's possible for him to learn how to do better next time and if I think therapy is the best way. After I answer both queries in the affirmative, he tells me that he'd never talked to a therapist before and, without thinking much about it, had believed that people who were in therapy were weak and couldn't make it on their own. But he'd been thinking about his own situation for a long time and decided that no matter what it meant, he needed help. He then tells me where he lives and asks if I can recommend a good therapist there. He also asks if I think it is possible to find a woman who is willing to accept him with all his medical and sexual problems. From what I can tell from his tone of voice, he seems surprised, but also happy, when I say I think it is entirely possible and, as evidence, point out that neither of his younger ladies had left him. He was the one who left.

I don't know if Ken contacted either of the two therapists whose names I gave him. But if he did, he may well have discovered that his situation is not unique, that grief over a lost relationship can be healed, that fears of inadequacy can be overcome, that one can learn better ways of keeping a relationship alive, and that there are people out there, women and men alike, who are willing to take a chance on someone with health problems and other issues. I hope he made the call.

Trudy

I met Trudy on an airplane returning to the Bay Area after a talk on the east coast. I was going over a draft chapter from this book and when she caught the title of it she asked what I was doing. We had an interesting conversation and she said, "I'd love to be able to help you with an interview but you wouldn't get much from me because there's nothing going on these days." I responded that "nothing going on" was interesting to me, and that was the beginning of our interview. Since I did not have my tape recorder with me, I took copious notes. Because of this, the interview lasted twice as long as usual, and we finished it in the San Francisco airport.

Trudy is 54 and has been married twice. The first marriage, to her college sweetheart, was "fantastic" for two years, but ended abruptly when he was killed in a motorcycle accident. She was devastated by her loss, almost had a nervous breakdown, and was so distraught that she fell into the arms of Sean, a man she thinks she would have recognized as a poor match in other circumstances. Although she stayed with Sean for 22 years and had two children with him, it was not, she says, a healthy union. Sean was a good provider, but he lived in a very different world from hers. His notion was a traditional one: he made the money and she, in return, was supposed to care for the house and children. She was also to provide nice dinners when he came home early enough to eat them, despite the fact that she, too, worked through most of the marriage and contributed significant income. Sean spent a great deal of time away from the home hanging out with his male buddies, all of whom he had known since high school or college. Spending time with Trudy seemed a chore to him after the first year of marriage and he hardly noticed the children at all. Talking intimately with Trudy, planning and having fun dates, cuddling, having leisurely sex at least occasionally—all these things that meant so much to her meant very little to him, or at least that's how he acted.

He did want sex and wasn't a bad lover, but as time went on, Trudy came to resent sex without a context of intimacy, sex that was more a physical release than an act of love. "He knew how to turn me on and get me off, I'll give him that," she acknowledges, "he was a good technician. At first that was enough, but I got tired of it. The orgasms became like huge sneezes, necessary and relaxing, but nothing to write home about. There was no love, no contact. It was very much like the casual sex I had after the divorce. Fine in the moment, but nothing to grab onto, nothing to feel good about the next day. We were fucking and getting off, but not connecting or bonding. I wanted more." As time went on, she found more and more reasons not to respond to his sexual overtures, which in turn made him even more distant.

Finally, with both children in college, Trudy decided she didn't have to live like this. She made enough money to pay her own way and she couldn't imagine a reason to stay with Sean. "My normal tendency, of course, would have been to talk to him about my dissatisfaction with the marriage and to work with him to find solutions. But I learned early on that talking was not his strong point. Besides, I don't think he wanted more than what we had. I was very unhappy and I believe that he was content. That's why he was so unhappy when I said I was leaving. He got real macho at first and said he wouldn't let me go, but after talking to his buddies he realized there was nothing he could do to stop me."

Trudy's experience in the world of singles has not been as rich as she had hoped for. "I wish I could say I am having a great time meeting all these interesting men and that I've found one I'm getting serious about, but that's not true. I spend a lot more time alone and with my girlfriends than I'd like. I don't get asked out half as much as I used to." There's another issue as well: "Although I'm still attractive and work hard at keeping my body in shape, I've started lying about my age. As soon as men hear an age starting with "50" their eyes glaze over. Amazing what an effect it has on them. So I've been saying I'm 48 or 49 for several years, or else I just refuse to give my age. I don't like to lie, but I'm not sure how else to handle this. Most of the men who take an interest in me are at least ten years my senior and I don't find them attractive. Typically, they're not in great physical shape—several had bellies so huge it was difficult to hug them—they're boring and lazy, they expect to be waited on, they're not interested in sex, or at least not much, and they know as much about relating as Sean did. This is not what I had in mind."

There's been some good sex since her divorce, but it was just sex, similar to what she had in her marriage. The combination of good sex plus romance and intimacy eludes her. Her longest relationship since the divorce has been four months. Otherwise, she's mainly had one-night or one-week stands.

That's unfortunate, she says, "Because I'm riper, juicier, and a better lover than I ever was. I have a great deal to give. Menopause hardly affected me. My desire is huge, my functioning is terrific—I'm quicker to orgasm than I ever was—and I'm ready and willing to do anything. One guy wanted me to tie him up and hit him with a little whip, another guy wanted me to pee on him, and another wanted to have me up the ass. I'd never done any of these things but I thought, why not give it a go? I did and except for the anal penetration, which hurt, we had some good times. [With tears streaming down her face] But as much as I enjoy naked bodies together, I wish I could find someone who appreciates all of me, what I can offer and who wants to talk to me. That's not asking too much, is it?"

Trudy exemplifies the situation of a great many unattached women over the age of 45. She's successful, attractive, and has learned much in her journey through life. Generally and sexually, she has a lot to offer. And she'd very much like to be in a healthy committed relationship. But her social life is much quieter than she wants. There simply aren't enough men to go around for mature women. An article in a special issue of *Scientific America* on men lays it out clearly: "At age 65, for every 100 American women, there are only 70 men" (1999, Vol 10, #2, p. 107). The differential is already present at age 45 and 50, and it just becomes more extreme as the years go by. Unfortunately, the situation is actually worse than is painted by this picture. When you take into account that there are a great many more homosexual men than lesbian women, that further reduces the pool of unattached men available for a woman such as Trudy, and many of the available heterosexual men are looking for women younger than Trudy.

I wish I had something to offer these women. It really isn't fair. Aside from Trudy's attractive physical appearance, there's a liveliness, perkiness, and quick intelligence about her that are real turn-ons. And yet the only solace I can offer Trudy is to point out that despite the odds, there are many women her age who have found satisfying relationships if they were willing to pay the price; finding out where the boys are and going there. I have spoken with several women who, for example, took up golf in midlife for the sole purpose of meeting men. Trudy mulls this over a moment, then assures me that this is a price she can easily pay.

Jacob

I feel the need to give an introduction to Jacob because unless you are like him or know someone like him you may find his story hard to believe. I don't find it surprising because over the years I have done therapy with scores of clients like him—men or women in their 40s, 50s, and 60s who haven't had a relationship or sex in many years, or in some cases ever. Such clients are different than Jacob, however, because they were concerned enough about their situation to seek help, something Jacob has not done. No one knows how many Jacobs there are and I am not suggesting there are many millions of them, but they may be more common than we would think. You don't have to go to a therapist's office to find them. I know that in my own extended family, there's a distant relative who is very much like Jacob. Now in his late 50s, he's never had a romantic relationship with anyone. His life is very simple: Monday through Friday he goes to the same job he's held since graduating from college, then goes shopping for his mother, followed by dinner and television at her place. Saturday and Sunday he sleeps late, watches videos, then back to mom's for dinner. I also had a lover some years ago whose sister was very similar.

Jacob is in his early 60s, in good health, successful in his demanding job, makes a good living, and hasn't had sex or a relationship since his divorce over 15 years ago. He says he's always been shy. Even as a child, he was happy to play with other kids, but only if they approached him. He was never one to initiate contact. As a result, he hardly dated in high school or college. Exceptions only rose when girls would ask him out.

It was in his last year in college that Randi, a girl in one of his classes, took an interest in him. She seemed to be everywhere he was—in the library, walking down the halls, in the coffee shop. They soon started dating and having sex. In time, they married and had three children.

Yet Jacob was never quite happy in the relationship. "It was such hard work," he explains. "Randi must be the world's biggest talker. It was nonstop. As soon as I got in the door, she'd start out with what her day was like, who did and said what to whom, all this trivial gossip. I just couldn't listen to all that stuff. Then she'd start in on me. How was my day? What did so and so say? What did I have for lunch and where? How was this and that going? I felt under assault. I just wanted peace and quiet, which is hard enough with young children around, but she was the worst."

Despite not having anything to compare it with, Jacob thinks the sex was good early on. "I really enjoyed it. Wonderful orgasms and I got a lot of pleasure making her come. It was terrific. But, as usual, it wasn't enough for her. She wanted us to talk during sex. How she felt, how I felt, if I liked this better than that, and on and on. She wanted me to talk dirty to her, which I thought was disgusting. And after sex, she'd have her usual list of questions: what I liked, what I'd like to do again, how much I loved her, that kind of thing."

As time went on, Jacob spent less time at home. He stayed at work later and later. He also started making excuses when Randi initiated sex, which effectively put an end to their sex life because he rarely initiated contact. The couple started bickering about all sorts of things and grew increasingly distant.

Randi tried many times without success to talk to Jacob about their growing estrangement and lack of sex. He listened but didn't know how to respond. The conversations solved nothing. She threatened divorce numerous times, but again Jacob says he didn't know how to respond. He loved his children and enjoyed his time with them, but he didn't like being with Randi. He just allowed events to take their course and was not surprised when one day Randi announced she had seen a lawyer and wanted a divorce.

In the 15 years since his divorce, Jacob has not had a single date with a woman. He is lonely, has no close friends, and most of his social life is with his three sons, although that is coming to an end because two are already away at college and the third will soon follow. He spends more time than is necessary at work (and he refuses to retire because he doesn't know what he would do with all the extra time), goes to sporting events, works a lot on his car (his only hobby), and visits porn sites on the Internet.

Jacob notices very few changes in his sexual desire and functioning. He thinks his desire is a bit lower than it was 20 years ago and maybe it takes him a bit longer to get aroused. His penis functions fine, and his orgasms are still very intense. Sometimes on a Sunday afternoon he may visit three or four different porn sites, masturbating and orgasming at each, all within a four-hour period. "In previous years," he says, "I sometimes would do it five or six times. Can't do that anymore, or at least I don't have the desire to." This is the only change in sexual interest and functioning he has noticed.

I ask Jacob directly if masturbation is an adequate substitute for partner sex. His response: "Masturbation is OK. I have great orgasms and get the release I want. But yeah, there's a lot about having someone else there that makes the whole thing richer and more interesting. I used to enjoy feeling Randi's body, the kissing, her hands on me, and all of that good stuff. I do miss it when I think about it. But you have to remember there's a price you pay for having these extra goodies. I can't just think about myself and how to give me the best possible orgasm. I have to think about her needs too. But the biggest price are the demands for talking and interacting before, during, and after. That was what killed me. I wonder if it's possible to have the goodies without having to give so much in return."

Jacob is not a happy man, but neither is he extremely unhappy. Perhaps wistful is the best way to describe his demeanor. "I've always had the dream of being married and involved with family. Even with Randi, there were many times when it felt really good to be married. Just seemed to be the right thing. I miss that part of it. And, to be honest, I have to say that somehow it doesn't seem right to be my age and single. This is not how I envisioned my life being. And it seems very adolescent and sad, getting sex by whacking off while surfing porn sites. But even with Internet dating services and personal ads, it's so hard for me to try to meet someone. And then I think of how much work is involved in a relationship. That's something I don't want to go through again. I have this fantasy now and again, that somehow I'll meet this woman who's more socially aggressive than me, she'll come find me, and we'll like each other, but she won't be half as demanding as Randi. Sure, we'll talk sometimes and we'll hold hands and have sex, but she won't always be after me to share and talk and discuss and converse. In a word, she'd leave me some space for myself. I wonder if that's really possible or if I'm just rationalizing my unwillingness to take any constructive steps."

Obviously, Jacob is not about to change. He will remain as he is unless, of course, some woman is willing to have a less than fully intimate relationship and is also willing to pursue him. The problem, however, is that the current situation is not the same as it was when Jacob and Randi were in college. There, everyone was visible and on display. No matter how shy a guy was, he had to show up at classes, in the library, on the campus, in the cafeteria, and so on. Randi first spotted Jacob in a class. But Jacob is a long way from college. Even if there is another Randi out there, it's difficult to imagine how she will meet him because he's no longer as visible. There are very few women where he works, he doesn't belong to any groups, clubs, or organizations, he won't even consider joining a singles group or checking out singles ads in the paper or on the Internet, and he's not about to visit health clubs, night clubs, or bars all of which are known as singles gathering places. If a new Randi is out there, she'll have to hire Sherlock Holmes to locate Jacob for her. Given this, I think it's unlikely Jacob's situation will change.

With Jacob, as with Jesse, we see an incredible fear of closeness. Jacob didn't even want to tell Randi about his day, or hear about hers, let alone talk about more intimate matters. Jesse, of course, handled it differently. He is not shy and he wants and needs a relationship. Yet because he can't tolerate too much closeness either, he manages the distance from within the relationship.

So we see some of the factors that characterize the non-lovers: fear of closeness, inability to communicate, inflexibility, anxiety, and few available potential partners. In the next chapter, we turn to people whose sex lives are considerably different from the ones we've read about here.

Chapter 6

The Lovers

I doubt that the vignettes in the last chapter made any readers jump up and exclaim, "Wow, I'd like a sex life like they're having!" That's as it should be; they leave a lot to be desired. Now that we've seen what doesn't work, it's time to meet seniors who do have satisfying sex. As I said in the Introduction, Lovers are the people I interviewed who rated their sex lives as "wonderful" or "very good" and supplied details to support these ratings. I deliberately did not use terms like "fantastic", "mind-blowing", or "out of this world". I have no doubt there are mature people who can honestly describe sex in these terms, but they aren't the people I was looking for. I was looking for sex that was achievable by most other mortals and for that goal "very good" and "wonderful" seemed to be the appropriate labels. Of the 145 people I interviewed, 80 are Lovers.

In the next several chapters, I describe the activities and attitudes that the Lovers have in common and that differentiate them from other interviewees. But in this chapter, I want to present the stories of three couples:

Wade and Betsy, who've been happily making love for 60 years; Cheri and Dan, who met in midlife and have been together three years; and Ben and Holly, who in midlife made some remarkable changes in their relationship. Given the spectrum of their experiences, I believe most readers will find that at least one of the couples has something to say to them.

Wade and Betsy

Wade and Betsy are the only couple I interviewed face to face. I was told by their daughter, whom I had previously interviewed, that I simply had to talk with her parents. They were willing but preferred a face-to-face interview to the phone. They sounded so charming in our phone conversation and their daughter had made such a compelling case that I flew to Arizona to meet with them in their home. I had broken my own rule about carrying out all interviews on the phone, but I did stick with the rule about interviewing partners separately.

Betsy and Wade met 63 years ago in college. It was love and lust at first sight. Wade felt that Betsy was, and still is, a very exciting woman, and she recalls that she was "mad" about him when they married a few years after they met. They hit it off from the start, and although they had to learn each other's ways, as each of them put it, there were no major misunderstandings or disasters, and Wade credits Betsy for teaching him how to communicate in an intimate relationship. Wade also reports that he had had a bad temper but that over the years, "I've learned to temper my temper. When we were first together, I once got very angry for some disappointment or another and she told me right off that that was not acceptable behavior. I started learning right then."

One thing that surprised Betsy was how close she and Wade became. "I was mad about him when I married him but I didn't expect him to become my best friend. I didn't know a man and a woman could be as intimate as I was with my women friends. But it happened and I'm so happy for it. He's a very unusual man. He's supported my interests, pursuits, and friendships. We shared everything. He'd get up with me at night when I had to nurse the babies."

Though they were both virgins when they met, Betsy and Wade enjoyed sex from the get-go and made it a priority in their lives. "I have always felt that we had a strong chemistry from the very beginning," says Betsy. She continues, "My husband makes my bells ring and the confetti fly." In the early years, they did a lot of experimenting with different locations, practices, and positions. Betsy notes: "We couldn't get enough. It was as if we were the first people to have discovered sex." When their two girls came along, they hired babysitters so they could take some weekends away from home. As Betsy notes, "I knew it was critical for our 'coupleness' for us to spend time alone together."

Interest in experimentation has declined over the years. These days they stick with the acts and places they know work best. As Wade puts it: "Sex is less wild, but not less good." Although sex has been a constant source of closeness and delight for them for 60 years, Betsy's sex drive has decreased somewhat in the last ten years, whereas, according to both of them, Wade's ardor has actually increased in that time.

This couple started scheduling dates for sex early in their relationship. One reason, says Betsy, is to ensure they actually have sex and not allow it to be put off because of chores, bills, and other obligations. Another reason for scheduling is to avoid rejections. She says it must be horrible to be sexually rejected and she doesn't want Wade to experience that. "So if he's interested and I'm just too tired, I suggest tomorrow morning or evening. That way I don't have to participate if I'm not in the mood and he doesn't have to feel rejected." Scheduling sex requires at least a modicum of communication, and Wade and Betsy have always been able to talk about lovemaking. Both assert they can say or request anything they want. And they are not shy about expressing their desires.

Both partners have experienced their share of health problems. Betsy has glaucoma, as well as an autoimmune disorder for which she takes Prednisone, and also vulvadynia for the last five years, a condition of unknown origin that causes severe sensitivity and irritation of the vulva. She has received a number of different treatments but so far nothing has helped. Because of this condition, the couple has been unable to have inter-course for five years. Their sexual contact consists entirely of manual and oral stimulation. Of this situation, Wade asserts, "We do what it's possible to do. I don't look at not having inter-course as a deficit or a deficiency. I'm grateful for what we had in the past and just as grateful for what we have now. The exact method or positions are not of primary importance to either of us, so long as we can have the intimate contact we crave and love so much."

Oh yes, and vibrator stimulation. Although Betsy says she has always enjoyed sex with her husband, she climaxed only about half the time. That is, until about twenty years ago when they discovered vibrators. With electrical stimulation she orgasms 100 percent of the time. Not only has the frequency of orgasm increased, so has the quality. She reports: "I attribute the fuller orgasms to the vibrator and also how we behave together. He holds me the way I like to be held. His touch makes me feel young and attractive and most desirable."

Wade had a stroke four years ago, which has left him weak on one side of his body. He also has some cardiac problems for which he takes several medicines. These medical issues have not affected his sexuality. Indeed, as noted earlier, his sexual desire has increased in recent years. He has had no problems having erections. In the last ten or so years, however, he has found he can't maintain an erection for as long as before. This is not a bad thing. Betsy explains that even before the vulvadynia, long intercourse was uncomfortable and sometimes painful, and she adds, "So him not being able to last as long has worked out well for us."

Wade and Betsy currently make love two or three times a month, more often when they're away from home. Both agree it would be even more frequent if not for the vulvadynia. Aside from the sex, there is a great deal of affectionate touching, even more than in earlier years. Wade is often the initiator because, as Betsy acknowledges, she often gets over-involved in daily tasks. "He's an incurable romantic," she says, "and the consummate lover." They frequently shower together, an activity that Wade says sometimes leads to hugging, which he finds exciting, which sometimes leads to sex.

Regarding what they get out of sex, here's what Betsy has to say: "I feel great and I know he feels great. There's also a sense of continuity that we have been doing this for over 60 years and ain't that great? I like the physical pleasure of orgasm. I also like the sweetness and peace of lying in bed together." Wade weighs in with this: "I get the pleasure of seeing her. She has soft skin, lovely breasts, a very beautiful figure. She's always been and still remains very exciting to me. I get to pleasure her, which gives me joy. I get pleasured and get tension release.

And sex reminds us, in the midst of the work-a-day world, how much we love each other. We're not just living in the same house. We're sharing a life together and we're very fortunate."

Given their ages and health, Wade and Betsy are aware that they probably don't have much time left together. Each expresses the wish to continue on as they have, sexually and otherwise, for as long as possible, and that the end come to both at the same time, that it be "sudden and over with a minimum of hassle and concern", and the least amount of suffering possible.

I don't know about you, but I believe they're doing pretty well for a couple in their mid-80s.

Cheri and Dan

Cheri is 55 years old, divorced after a 20-year marriage, and has two children, now grown up. She has been with her current lover, Dan, for three years.

In her marriage, Cheri says that both she and her ex-husband were relatively inexperienced (she notes that she didn't try oral sex until after they were married) and "learned about sex from the ground up". She says she has always liked sex and had a good sexual relationship with her husband "within the confines of what we both brought to the table". They actually did better with sex than with the rest of the relationship. After the children came along, there were conflicts regarding taking care of the children and nurturing the adult relationship; somehow this business was never sorted out and the couple grew more distant until they finally decided to end the marriage.

Since her divorce, Cheri has had a number of relationships with men, some very short and one lasting over two years. She thinks she's learned about herself, sex, and relationships in every relationship she's had and she's a better person for the experiences. "I learned to lower my expectations and be more realistic. There's only so much another person can do for you. No one else can make me happy. That's my responsibility. I learned about the importance of communication, of really talking and not holding things in, especially talking about things that are the hardest to talk about. Even though it's difficult and part of you doesn't want to do it, you have to, otherwise, the relationship will wither."

Cheri thinks she was very lucky to have met Dan. She knew he was the one the first time she laid eyes on him at a community event. "When I spotted him for the first time, he looked like the person I had been wanting to meet, so when it turned out he was as wonderful as he is—very educated and intellectual, very funny, and the most imaginative and creative man I've ever met—I knew it was him." With him she is enjoying the best relationship and the best sex she's ever had. She sums up her relationship like this: "We really admire and respect one another and are just happy with one another's company. We love to talk, touch, and do things together. We both have our feet on the ground, we've learned a lot in our journeys through life, and we both feel extremely fortunate to have come together."

Cheri's health is excellent and everything about sex with Dan is the best ever. She gives much of the credit to her partner but he, she says, gives most of it to her. Maybe, she acknowledges, it's both of them. Her desire has increased and so has the amount of sex she's having. It's always been easy for her to get aroused: "For me, it's always been a Pavlovian response. Once I'm in sync with a lover, then a small kiss, a pat, even a few words, and I'll be turned on." With Dan, it's even quicker and stronger: "Obviously I'm older but my sexual response with him is light years beyond anything I've experienced before."

One thing Cheri learned while dating was that despite her fondness for sex and her quick turn-ons, it's difficult for her to orgasm outside of the context of a trusting, caring, and committed relationship. She had several three-to-four month relationships after her divorce and discovered that orgasms were difficult to attain.

With Dan, Cheri is having the most orgasms ever, the most diverse, the quickest, and the most intense. "This is by far the most intense. It's so intense sometimes that I feel like I'm going to faint. I can have orgasms with just penetration and no clitoral contact and orgasms just with him caressing my nipples. I didn't even know I could do such things. I may have been capable of doing this 25 years ago, but I just didn't have a partner who knew how to work with me on it. I hadn't experienced a lot of things that I'm now experiencing. I had no idea that I could have a bazillion multiple orgasms, like over and over and over for as long as we are willing to continue stimulation. It had never entered my mind that such a thing was possible." Cheri is orgasmic 100 percent of the time she masturbates and 100 percent of the time with Dan, although she reports that she's hardly masturbated at all since meeting Dan.

By most standards, this couple has sex frequently. "We have sex about 7 times a week, but that's not once a day. We don't live together and don't see each other every day. We spend most of the weekend together and maybe two other nights. We might have sex four times on the weekend, sometimes three times in one day." Cheri reports that sex is very important to them; "We're willing to put other things aside to make time for lovemaking." When I asked about their sexual communication, she said it was excellent, that they talk about erotic things before, during, and after sex and that no topic is taboo. Summing up their communication, she put it this way: "We laugh and talk and screw at the same time."

Very aware of the aging process, Cheri is especially pleased with how Dan responds to her body. "My partner is happy with the way my body feels and looks. He talks about it and he likes to watch me when I don't have any clothes on. He's always giving me compliments about my body. I'm more critical. Obviously, I have an older body and an older face. I walk past a mirror and look at myself and think, Oh my gosh, those flabby arms. They're so flabby and floppy, especially on the back side. I'm embarrassed to wave at anyone or raise my hand. I see things that didn't used to be there and I think of them negatively. But since these don't affect him, they don't bother me as much. I feel much better about my physical appearance because of him."

Like most of the other Lovers, Cheri couldn't think of anything about sex she doesn't like, except possibly the "unavoidable wet spot on the bed". When I asked what she would wish for in her love and sex life, she couldn't think of anything she wanted to change: "I just want it to keep on going like this forever."

This couple plans to marry in the next year, an event both are anticipating with much enthusiasm. Cheri is looking forward to the challenges that living together will bring to their relationship and especially to sleeping with Dan every night of the week. "It will be so nice," she says, "not to have these tearful leave-takings. Even though I know I'll see him again in a few days at most, I still miss him a lot when we're on different sides of the Bay at night. I even miss his body odor. I know many people will hear that as a bad thing—I mean, body *odor*—but it's crucial to me. I love his scent; if I didn't, I don't know that I could love him and have fantastic sex with him. When he's not here at night, I sniff his pillow to see if I can get a whiff. It'll be a lot easier when he's here and I can just lean over and inhale deeply."

Molly and Sam

Seven years ago Molly and Sam, then in their mid-50s, had an epiphany. They both realized that their nine-year marriage was heading in the same direction as their disastrous first marriages and that unless something were done, and soon, they would end up divorced or, just as bad, stuck forever in a barely functional marriage. As they took stock of their union, they saw it was in shambles, which isn't surprising since they both came from very distressed families. Sam was depressed and resentful, Molly was often angry. Neither could ask for what he or she wanted in bed or out; neither gave much feedback on what they were getting; Molly couldn't initiate sex; sex became less and less frequent; Sam had no desire and an erection problem as well; and they didn't have any good ways of dealing with differences.

They decided to get counseling. This was, they say, the best decision they ever made as a couple. The therapy changed almost everything about their marriage, from how they talk and express feelings to how they make up after conflict. It also affected how and how often they make love. They are, they say, "poster children for the effectiveness of marital/sexual therapy", and they want everyone to know just how well it worked for them.

They rate the general quality of their marriage in the four years since therapy ended as "very happy to fabulous", and both rate communication as excellent. Molly's take on this: "Being much better at communicating with Sam has made the relationship more satisfying than any other relationship I've ever had. We've gotten through some difficult issues, we've learned to trust each other more in ways I never thought existed. There is much less tension. We're much more able to complain to each other about small things. We used to be terrified of any disagreement and avoided them at all costs because any disagreement could lead to 'the big one' and then we would lose each other. Our relationship is better than I thought a relationship could be. I didn't realize how much intimacy and trust and support I could get from another human being."

Sam describes a crucial aspect of therapy for him: "Learning to talk more, to expose myself by being more open and thereby getting closer to my wife. Even though this was difficult for me, I learned I didn't need to defend my psychological perimeter." This had led to important developments in Sam's life even outside the marriage. "The mix of my friends has moved away from a majority of men to a majority of women because the women I know are more willing to talk. And my overall feeling about friends has become more positive than it used to be."

Sam made an important discovery about having a good relationship: "I realized I didn't have to do everything my wife did. We could have separate interests and pursue them separately. Now I feel like I lead a richer life, more like a life and a half; not only do I have my experiences, but I also have my wife's because we always share our separate experiences at the end of the day."

Regarding sexual desire, Molly reports that she is more conscious of what she wants than she used to be: "When I was younger, I was not sure my sexual desire was really mine. I didn't go into sex for fulfillment; I was much more focused on being desirable." Now, however, she's much more conscious of her desires and of Sam's as well. Sam's interest in sexual frequency has increased to the point where it now pretty much matches his wife's. He adds something of note: "My interest in intensity and in extending the time we spend having sex have increased. When I was younger and wanted sex, I was looking for maybe a 20-minute encounter. Now I want to luxuriate in it, I am more interested in sex being a two-hour transaction."

There is a lot more cuddling and physical affection, in addition to sexual contact once or twice week, which feels about right to both. Molly and Sam both report an increased intensity in orgasm and Molly's orgasms have become more reliable than ever. "I seldom have orgasm from intercourse alone, but it's a pretty sure thing with oral stimulation."

Sex has become a priority for this couple. They often schedule it and, as Molly says: "We give ourselves lots of time. We don't insist that it lead to intercourse. We play around a lot, we talk to each other. We do a lot of hand manipulation, stroking, and fondling. We hug and touch each other outside of bed a lot during the day. We are comfortable with each other physically."

Molly has become much more willing to give Sam direction and feedback, which earlier she was reluctant to do and for a while he was resistant to. "Now," he says, "I appreciate hearing it. She is more willing to recognize her right to enjoy herself. She recognizes I want to give her pleasure, and if she tells me how, I can do a better job of it. I'm happy for the guidance."

Sam attributes the change in their sex life to what happens outside the bedroom: "The ways we honor each other, respect each other, evidence our interest in one another's lives, and the way we hold each other when we cry, or share happiness. We discuss movies, books, plays, or go to the theater or out to dinner. We are getting closer to each other. We are beginning to understand each other more. We are beginning to recognize that we frequently surprise the other person, that we are not predictable. We are not judging each other. We are not insisting that the other achieves our goal. We split all household chores. We take each other less for granted."

Regarding what he gets out of sex with Molly, Sam puts it like this: "It makes my whole life better. There is the pleasure of the moment. There is a reassurance that I'm still alive." Molly: "I get lots of physical satisfaction with the orgasm and feeling close. I get a sense of connection to my husband. I get the pleasure of expressing my affection for him in a way that he really appreciates. It's like renewing your vows. I get a sense of recommitment when we make love."

All is not perfect for this couple. Molly and Sam acknowledge that their sexual communication isn't all they would like it to be. They would like to feel more confident and relaxed stating preferences during lovemaking. But they're working on it.

Although Sam's erection situation is much improved from what it was before counseling, his erections are not as reliable as when he was younger. Yet both he and Molly say it really isn't a problem. Each time they make love, they do what's possible and what they like. Intercourse isn't necessary for her orgasm or his. And there's something else. Like almost every woman I interviewed, Molly is concerned about her aging body and sometimes wonders if she is sexually attractive to her husband. "His compliments and assurances in this regard are very important to me, as is his pointing out that his body is changing too."

During the course of their therapy and making the changes already mentioned, Molly and Sam were faced with a difficult decision. Molly's mother, toward whom Molly felt quite ambivalent, was becoming unable to care for herself. Because of dementia, a serious heart condition, and arthritis, she needed help in performing everyday tasks. It was difficult for her to get out of bed and to the bathroom, and she had lapses of memory. One day she forgot she had left the burner on in the kitchen and almost burned the apartment down. She was not receptive to the idea of moving, but if she did, she wanted to be with Molly and Sam, both of whom had started visiting her more and more frequently to care for her needs.

Molly felt obligated to do something for her ailing mother, but because of her mother's neglect of her as a child, did not want to be too close to her. Sam was willing to do whatever Molly desired, but he really didn't want her mother in their house. He felt it would disrupt the progress they were making on their marriage; in fact, he believed that the increased visiting was already getting in their way.

The couple spent several weeks going over the options and their feelings, both alone and with their therapist. Molly felt some guilt about putting her mother in a nursing home, as did her husband, but that's what she really wanted. Finally, they agreed on this solution as being the best for them. They would promise her mother that at least one of them would visit once a week and they would deal with their guilt if it arose again.

Molly's mother was understandably upset by their decision and argued against it as strenuously as she could, but she soon understood that they would not budge. None of the manipulative skills she had used so successfully on Molly as a child worked. After having them repeat a number of times that they would hold to their promise of visiting once a week, she finally consented.

Molly did have periods of guilt when her mother called up crying from the nursing home they found for her. But she dealt with these with Sam and sometimes the therapist. Looking back, Molly and Sam view their decision regarding her mother as the best one they could have chosen and have no regrets about it.

I was able to contact this couple two years after interviewing them and was pleased to hear that things continued to improve. As Molly put it, "I never, ever, would have imagined I could have something so good and so complete; I didn't even know it existed for anyone. Sam is my best friend, my playmate, my support, my joy, and my lover, and things are going wonderfully in each area. I know I speak for both of us in saying that we're very happy, happier than ever before. All we want is for things to continue this way for as long as possible."

Some common questions about The Lovers

You will meet more Lover couples in the following chapters, especially the one entitled "What's Health Got To Do With It?" but now I turn to some of the questions I have been asked about the research on which this book is based.

Are Lovers perfect people or do they have perfect relationships?

Some people have said the Lovers must be perfect people. One man said they sounded like space aliens; he couldn't believe human beings could be this way. A woman client who has been holding on to resentment toward her husband for over a decade couldn't believe that real people could so easily let go of negative emotions. She thought everyone was like her, holding on to resentments for dear life.

Although Lovers share some characteristics, the material presented in the following chapters shows that they also differ in many ways. In some of the Lovers' relationships, debating and even brief arguments are common; in others, such interactions are rare or nonexistent. All Lovers seem to be talkers, but there is more conversation in some relationships than in others. As far as personal styles go, I ran into quite a few. Some of the Lovers seemed to really have themselves together. They're about as fit and grounded as is possible at this stage of life. But not all the Lovers are this way. Some occasionally have depressive episodes; some are more reclusive and others more social than is helpful or healthy for them; some are big risk takers while others are quite cautious; some are more aware of control issues than is probably necessary or beneficial; and some are anxious to some extent or another.

Even though all of the Lovers have their own styles and idiosyncracies, none of them, as far as I can determine, are psychotic or even close to what's usually considered crazy. They are well grounded in reality. They understand themselves, their partners, their families, what they want, and what needs to be done to get and keep what they want.

It's important as you read on to keep in mind that when I compare Lovers with other couples, I'm talking about differences of degree. I do not want to imply that Lovers talk a lot, and other couples don't talk at all. It is simply that my data strongly suggest that Lovers generally talk more than other couples, and in more positive ways.

All the Lovers I interviewed made it clear that neither they nor their partners were perfect. Virtually all of them pointed out things in their marriage or sex life that could be better. But the point is that the partners have made peace with their own and their partner's shortcomings or idiosyncracies. They do not allow these things to drive them crazy. They look at what they have instead of what they don't have, and they make the most of it. All of these people had come to a place where they realized that their partner and their relationship was good enough. As one of them said, "Being happy in a relationship is a choice or decision." Since there's good and not so good in every relationship, one can choose what part to focus on. Concentrate on the not so good, and you'll feel not so good most of the time. Concentrate on the good, and you'll feel good most of the time. That's what it comes down to.

Were Lovers born that way?

Some, like Betsy and Wade, had great relationships almost from day one, but most Lovers, as you have already surmised from the interview excerpts, had anything but ideal relationships for most of their lives. Some didn't find happiness until their second or even third marriages; some of them had years of difficulty before things came together. Some learned from their unsuccessful experiences; others found answers in some kind of therapy, alone or with a partner. The good news is that there's hope for almost anyone who desires a better relationship. Midlife or later is not too late.

Did lovers have especially good role-models or education regarding romance and sexuality?

If Lovers weren't born that way, perhaps their parents were excellent exemplars who by their behavior and words provided great educations in intimacy. While this was true for a small number of Lovers—an example is Betsy and Wade's daughter, a Lover in her own marriage and the person who referred me to her parents—it wasn't the case for most. Most of the Lovers had the same laments as Non-lovers: their parents had middling to horrible relationships, never touched, and sex was never mentioned in the house. In some households, things were even worse, with the parents abusing one another and putting forth very antisexual messages. The fact that most of the Lovers did not achieve fabulous intimacy and eroticism until midlife or later, after numerous years and/or relationships, also suggests that what they accomplished was the result of their own efforts and not something that had been modeled for them in childhood.

I'm not saying that good modeling and sensitive, accurate sex education for children has no effect (on the contrary, I strongly believe they have a powerful positive influence), but rather that in my sample there were so few people who got either one that it's impossible to draw any conclusions. That little was given by the parents of these interviewees is not surprising given that I interviewed only people over the age of 45. We might find something different in a younger sample whose parents grew up with more sexually liberal ideas.

Are Lovers too close to or too dependent on their partners?
To some people, the closeness of the Lovers sounds unseemly and somehow bad or wrong. One man even declared that to him they sounded like "pampered, dependent wimps". In any case, I did not see any evidence that the Lovers I interviewed are too dependent on their partners. By and large, Lovers are independent and successful women and men. Yet they have chosen to spend a significant portion of their time and energy with their mate, not because they have to or because of some

emotional problem. It's simply that being together gives them what they want most. And because they are so happy and lively, Lovers are attractive to, and sought after by, others whether for committees or social events. Men and women shopping for new romantic partners or affairs also seek them out. But Lovers often choose not to participate in the social events because they'd rather be alone with each other and they typically avoid extra-relationship entanglements because they are so content with what they already have.

What do Lovers look like?

Please keep in mind that I did not meet most of the people I interviewed. I know them only through phone calls. But since I started out with people I did know, I can respond to this question. Lovers look pretty much like other people with one exception; they are happy and it shows. Lovers come in all shapes and sizes and of those who I did meet in person, there was not a preponderance of beautiful men and women. These are not movie stars or models. They are ordinary looking people who have achieved something extraordinary in their relationships.

The most impressive physical characteristic of the Lovers is that they're often smiling. What they have in their kitchens, living rooms and bedrooms shines through in their facial expressions and demeanors. I believe this finding is very encouraging. Neither you nor your partner have to measure up to some particular standard of looks or physique to be a Lover. However you look is good enough.

What do Lovers actually do?

Lovers do not all act the same in lovemaking. Some are traditional; some more creative and adventuresome. Some stick pretty much to the conventional foreplay, intercourse, afterplay routine. Others spend more time with oral sex, anal sex, sex toys, erotica, and light S & M. Some share or act out fantasies and talk dirty. Others do not, or not much. Although virtually all of them talk during and about sex, some do so a great deal more than others. Some typically use marijuana or wine before sex, most do not. Some are forever looking for new places, acts, and positions, others seem content with a less varied menu.

I did not hear from any of the Lovers about any new or special techniques or positions. You will be disappointed if you expected that their excellent sex is based on such 'secrets'. There are only so many convex and concave surfaces on the human body, and only so many protuberances and places to put them, and most of these are well known.

There is one common characteristic in sexual behavior among Lovers that deserves a few words here, and several examples will be given in the following chapters. The Lovers are very flexible and open to change. Regardless of their preferences and regardless of how they are accustomed to going about making love, if something occurs that makes change necessary or desirable, they will make the alterations quickly and without whining or finger pointing.

Another common characteristic among the Lovers is an emphasis on afterplay, the activities after the sexual acts are over. The Non-lovers didn't have a lot to say about this, but almost all the Lovers mentioned how the cuddling, talking, laughing, and giggling afterward adds to their whole sense of well-being and happiness. It makes sense. These people have a good time with or without sex, as well as before, during, and after sex.

The 'keys' that make these people Lovers will be discussed in the following chapters. You'll soon discover there's nothing secret about them. In a sense, everyone knows them, but only a few have the incentive, assertiveness, courage, and determination to practice them regularly. Those people are the Lovers.

Do Lovers have affairs?

While a number of other couples I interviewed and clients I've seen over the years have engaged in extracurricular activities with people other than their partners, Lovers apparently do not. Not one Lover I interviewed admitted to an affair. I can't swear to the veracity of this finding because affairs are one place where people often lie. Nonetheless, the evidence is pretty clear: Lovers rarely or never have sex with people other than their partners. And it makes sense: they have great relationships and great sex at home, so why go elsewhere, especially for something that's bound to be so disappointing? And why risk something so precious? Len, a well-traveled Lover said the following:

 Despite my age [close to 80], I'm often in places and situations where I meet attractive women who let it be known one way or another that they're available for some hanky-panky. I'm sometimes tempted—they're much younger than me, quite sexy and attractive, and they already know I'm not available for anything more than a night or two. I believe I could have sex with them without emotional strings and without it having much meaning. But when I think of how much it would hurt my wife and how betrayed she would feel, I lose my appetite for the whole thing. And there's no way I could keep it a secret. We're just too open with each other. She'd know right away that I was holding something back. I couldn't hurt my beloved this way, and I haven't.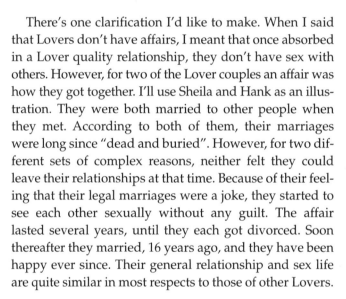

There's one clarification I'd like to make. When I said that Lovers don't have affairs, I meant that once absorbed in a Lover quality relationship, they don't have sex with others. However, for two of the Lover couples an affair was how they got together. I'll use Sheila and Hank as an illustration. They were both married to other people when they met. According to both of them, their marriages were long since "dead and buried". However, for two different sets of complex reasons, neither felt they could leave their relationships at that time. Because of their feeling that their legal marriages were a joke, they started to see each other sexually without any guilt. The affair lasted several years, until they each got divorced. Soon thereafter they married, 16 years ago, and they have been happy ever since. Their general relationship and sex life are quite similar in most respects to those of other Lovers.

What about physical abuse?

I did not ask specifically about physical abuse in the interviews but it came up a number of times in the responses of Non-lovers and also of Lovers regarding previous relationships. None of the Lovers reported physical abuse in their current relationships in recent times. Two mentioned some pushing and shoving many years ago in their current relationships, but both took it as a wake-up call and sought professional help.

As far as the prior relationships of Lovers and the prior as well as current relationships of Non-lovers, a fair amount of abuse was reported, about as much I suspect that we would find in the general middle-class population. I heard as many reports of women slapping, kicking, or punching men, or throwing objects at them, as of men doing the same.

It makes sense that physical violence is nonexistent, or virtually so, among the Lovers. Like affairs, physical abuse (as well as emotional abuse) is contrary to too many of their values. Besides, as we will see in the next chapters, these couples have proven ways of dealing with conflict and anger. They rarely if ever reach the place where they or their feelings are out of control.

What about sex differences?

In recent years we've heard a lot about Venus and Mars, about the differences between men and women. A lot of what we've heard is common sense—a lot is nonsense. My research was not targeted at sex differences, but one observation was obvious. Among the Non-lovers there was ample evidence of the expected differences between women and men. Jessie and Barb are excellent examples. He is distant, fearful of being too close, doesn't want too much touching or too much sex. She, on the other hand, wants more talking, touching, and sex. Because he's the man of the family, he gets his way. During Jacob's marriage to Randi, his job was to bring in the family income. Her job was to take care of the children and home.

Among the Lovers, there were plenty of individual differences; however, between the sexes, differences were not pronounced. These relationships were in most ways based on equality. Men did so-called women's work and played so-called women's roles; women did men's work and played men's roles. Wade is the romantic person in his marriage to Betsy. She often becomes so involved in her tasks that she forgets about intimate talk, touching, and sex. He has to remind her. But because they value and respect one another, he can let her know when he'd like an erotic break. Their communication is person to person, not stereotype to stereotype.

Among the Lovers, both partners initiate intimate conversation, affection, and lovemaking. Practices and positions are determined by mutual preference and negotiation if necessary. There is no rule in force that men should initiate, that men should be on top, or that they orchestrate sex. Either partner can and does do any and all of these things depending on how they feel at the moment. Each partner feels free to bring up complaints and problems in the relationship or lovemaking.

Chores are often done together, for example, shopping for food, cleaning the bathroom, making the beds. If not, they're done by whoever is available and has the competence. Generally, the doing of household chores is among the top reasons for arguments in American couples, so it is noteworthy that among the Lovers this topic just didn't come up as an issue. Each person does what needs to be done. If there are dirty clothes on the floor, the first one to see them picks them up. If there's no milk, the person who first notices it buys milk.

Individual preferences play a much larger part in the interactions than do conventions. For instance, in my relationship with Marilynne, I detest making the bed, mostly because I feel that I don't do it well. I don't think I've once made the bed and felt good about the results. So when the bed is a mess, Marilynne straightens it. But I do almost all the food shopping, except when we do it together, and most of the cooking. We both take out the garbage and recycling. The laundry is done by whoever first notices that there's a load that needs washing. And so it is with most of the Lovers.

I believe the Lover's relationships are a somewhat different kind of relationship on the American landscape. While traditional rules are not necessarily vehemently criticized or even discussed, empiricism is the ruling principle. Rooted in love, respect, and equality, each Lover couple develops practices that best work for their situation. How well these rules fit with what their parents did or do, or what the neighbors do, or what the experts say is not a consideration. Simply put: they do what works.

Chapter 7

Relating

In this chapter and those that follow, I address the difference between Lovers and other couples to determine what the Lovers do to make possible their enduring romances. In order to be as accurate as possible, and to mitigate the potential for erroneous conclusions, it is necessary to have comparison or control groups.

An interesting aside: One of the silliest mistakes ever made in medicine was made precisely because of a lack of understanding about the need for controls. Starting in the mid-1700s, the idea gained prominence that masturbation caused mental illness. Masturbatory insanity, which is what it was called, was promulgated by the medical profession in Western Europe and the United States. The attendant publicity was enough to scare those who did masturbate and to deflect attention from looking seriously at the real causes of mental illness.

The reason, the only one ever mentioned, that people thought masturbation led to insanity was the observation that mental patients in asylums did indeed masturbate, which was true. But no one thought of looking at the masturbatory behavior of those not in asylums, or realizing that there's nothing much else to do in such places, and that the patients have absolutely no privacy. Whatever a patient does there will be done in public and therefore be open to observation. The rational basis for masturbatory insanity would have been questioned had anyone observed or even asked about the solitary sexual behavior of people other than inmates, had they put normal people in asylum-like situations to check on what behavior changes were introduced, or had they given patients more privacy and the wherewithal to engage in other activities —see plays, listen to concerts, write letters, read books, play chess, engage in sports, and so forth.

With this backdrop, I realized I needed couples who did not have extraordinary sex to compare with those who did. If it turned out that individuals in both groups tended to sleep seven to eight hours a night, that probably meant that amount of sleep was not a factor in explaining great sex. Control groups would definitely help.

Fortunately, I had not one but two comparison groups. One group consisted of couples I had interviewed who had not rated their sex lives as highly as the Lovers had. The other group comprised sex therapy clients, people who had consulted me precisely because sex was a problem. So, the advantage was in having a way to measure outstanding differentials between groups. If it was the case, for example, that the vast majority of Lovers watched only a little television—less than two hours per week—whereas the vast majority of the other groups watched at least four hours a day, then like it or not, believe it or not, the amount of time gazing at the tube was correlated with the maintenance of happy sexuality, and it would be my job to try to figure out how.

As I began my comparisons and analysis, it was immediately clear that the gods were with me. I didn't have to go scrounging around for small differences. Huge differences leaped out at me from the transcripts. Lovers and Non-lovers were different in significant, logical, and understandable ways. There were specific things we could learn from the Lovers. By following their leads, we could develop sex lives more like theirs and, perhaps, be as contented.

The first lesson: have a great relationship

According to the Lovers I interviewed, if you want good sex, the first prerequisite is a good relationship. Virtually all of the men and women who reported having great sex also reported being in relationships that were wonderful or very good. Most of them, women and men alike, spontaneously offered that their spouse was their good friend or, more typically, their best friend: "She's my best friend, my colleague, my lover", "He's my soulmate and best friend."

A woman in her 60s who has been married over 30 years put it this way:

> " I think our great sex stems from our excellent rela-
> tionship. We love each other and want to do nice
> things for each other. Sex is just one of the arenas
> where we get to do these nice things. I want to please
> him, he wants to please me, and we do. We share our
> lives, we share our pleasures. "

A male Lover in his late 50s who has been married for
almost over 25 years put it succinctly: "The quality of our
lovemaking is much better now, because the quality of
our relationship has improved in the last 12 to 15 years."

The difference a good relationship can make in one's
sex life is dramatically showcased in the report of Stan,
whom we met in Chapter 5. Now 76 years old, he had an
excellent marriage with his first wife until her death nine
years ago. This marriage was about as good as it gets.
"We could talk about anything," he says, but talk wasn't
necessary after a while. "After so many years together,
you learn each other's ways pretty good. I could finish
her sentences and she could finish mine. But if anything
new came up, if we had to thrash it out, we could and we
did." It wasn't always this good and there were some
rocky times in the early years. Over time, however, they
both became more accepting and tolerant. "I didn't get as
upset when she got upset and when she was irritable, I
guess I mellowed over time. More and more, I realized
how lucky I was to have her and how wonderful what we
had together was."

Their sex life mirrored their marriage. It was, he says:

> ... always wonderful. It was an important part of our lives that we always made a place for. Even when the kids were young, we always arranged private time for just the two of us. After the kids moved on, we had my father living with us for several years until his death, and then we went through the same thing with her mother. Even though caring for them and dealing with their needs and demands was often time-consuming and exhausting, we continued our habit of arranging private time just for us. We loved pleasing each other. I think that was because we loved each other so much. We liked each other's bodies—looking, touching, kissing, pleasing.

In this marriage, they made love about twice a week in their late 50s and early 60s, until her illness made this impossible. But as we also saw in Chapter 5, the quality of Stan's second marriage is poor and, not surprisingly, so is the lovemaking.

The majority of Lovers said that their relationships had improved considerably as they approached or were in the midst of middle age. This comment is typical:

> At the beginning and actually for a number of years after, we had heavy-duty fights, especially about in-laws. But about ten years ago we both realized fighting didn't work, so we started introducing humor into our more delicate discussions and that's helped tremendously. It's also helped that I've become far less focused on myself. I came to understand there are other ways besides my way of thinking, there are other points of view. I try to see things through my wife's eyes and her perspective. Maybe she has some good ideas too. I feel it's part of the maturation

> process: more acceptance and tolerance of other points of view. And the quality of sex has become much better as the quality of the relationship has improved.

Middle age seems to be a natural time in the life cycle for both men and women to mature, to develop tolerance and acceptance, to come to what Molly, whom we met in the last chapter, called "a new and superior model of relating".

After listening to all of the interviews on tape and also reading the transcripts, I grouped the characteristics of the Lover's relationships into a number of categories that differentiated them from the not-so-happy people I interviewed and the not-so-happy clients of the same age I see in therapy.

Before getting to these attributes, however, I want to share the conclusion of a review of a number of studies on marriage over time:

> A well-documented decline in marital satisfaction often begins with the birth of the first child. ... Lower levels of marital satisfaction persist while there are children in the home. ... There is, however, evidence of a 'devitalization' of marriage over time that occurs whether children are in the home or not. Both husbands and wives report a drop in the pleasing things their partners do for them and in the time they spend together doing leisure activities. Couples become less affectionate over time and less expressive of their positive feelings toward one another (Prager, 1995, p. 145).

The humorist Dave Barry captures the specifics in this quote from his book, *Big Trouble*:

> He told her about how he and Patti met in college and fell in love and went dancing all the time, and then Matt was born and that was wonderful, but they didn't dance as much, but they swore they would, one of these days, when Matt got a little older, but they never did, and after while they stop talking about going dancing, in fact they stop talking about pretty much anything, and they made love only when neither of them could immediately think of an excuse not too, which happened very rarely, because any excuse would do, starting with 'I'm kinda tired tonight', which they both were, every night. He talked about the slow, agonizing slide down the slope of divorce..." (1999, p. 73).

The alert reader will have noticed that these two quotes contradict what I said in Chapter 4 about people gaining more control over their emotions with age and becoming more positive and less negative. The contradiction is more apparent than real because we're talking about different people. In many long relationships, things do get worse with time. But there are exceptions and here are the ways the Lovers manage to beat the odds. I believe the crux of the matter is reflected in the phrase I heard over and over from the Lovers: "We take good care of each other."

Like, respect, and being together

The two terms, "like" and "respect", were brought up spontaneously by most interviewees and they were clearly positive in discussing their partners and their relationships. There's no question about it: Lovers really like each other. Lovers emphasize their partner's strengths—thoughtfulness, understanding, intelligence, sense of humor, gentleness, sexiness, and on and on. A woman in her late 50s, for example, said her husband was the "most interesting person I've ever met. He knows about science, arts, history, just about everything. No matter what the topic, he always has something fascinating to add. I'd rather talk to him than anyone else on earth."

The Lovers were willing to discuss their partner's weaknesses and shortcomings, but it was always in a positive and accepting way. This was in sharp contrast to the unhappy couples I interviewed and also the couples I see in therapy. With these two groups, the complaints and criticisms—often accompanied by contempt, the single most powerful predictor of marital unhappiness and dissolution (Gottman, 1999)—come gushing out at the first opportunity and rarely is a positive note heard. From the Lovers, however, there was not a hint of contempt. Instead, there was compassion and acceptance.

Most of the time Lovers think quite positively about their mates and look forward to being with them. When they are together, they are present and understand what a gift they have. I detected no sex differences in this regard. Both men and women were equally desirous of being with their sweethearts, of talking with them, touching them, and sharing the rest of life's bounty. In most unhappy couples, on the other hand, there is often one partner who does not much want to be with the other. As one of my divorced interviewees said of his marriage, "For 20 years she kept pushing for more time together, more talking, more affection, and more sex, and for 20 years I kept running away from her."

Because they like each other so much, Lovers enjoy their time together no matter what they are doing. One man said it succinctly: "We could have a good time sitting on the curb and talking." Many of the Lovers spontaneously reported that they enjoy even the most mundane tasks such as shopping, cleaning the house, or paying bills. A woman in her 60s added this: "We're always doing nice things for each other. I suggest we eat at places I know he likes and bring him little presents I know he'll enjoy. He does the same for me." These people are having a good time.

Lovers give time with their partners very high priority. A woman whose 20-year marriage was not always this good says that what helped improve it was "making it our number one priority". Other Lovers agree. You can't have a wonderful marriage if you're putting other things first. Another woman who has had a wonderful live-in relationship for 15 years after two divorces says that she's learned a lot about relating from her experiences and one of the most important lessons she learned from her current partner was to put the relationship first. "I don't do all the things I used to do, I've given up a lot of work-related activities so I can make this the most important thing in my life. Much to the chagrin of my friends, I'm much less social than I was." Other couples also reported that their social lives had to be sacrificed to some extent to make more time and energy available for their relationship and that not all their friends and relatives were thrilled by this.

Because they like each other so much, Lovers want to spend time together. They also know you can't be single in a relationship, that the only way to be in a good relationship is by relating, which takes time and energy, and often planning as well. They are more than willing to pay the price. In order to have quality time together, the Lovers resort to a variety of strategies and rituals. Some, for instance, take regular vacations, just the two of them. Some have special times (an afternoon and evening each week, for example) when they don't accept social engagements and don't do work or answer the phone. For others it's as simple as not answering the phone during dinner so they can catch up with one another. Yes, it's true, many of the Lovers regularly have meals together. Others have a cutoff point in the evening, 9 or 10 p.m., after which there is no work, no playing with the computer, and no answering the phone. One way or another, they preserve their time together.

I emphasize eating together simply because everyone has to eat and mealtime is a wonderful time to connect, whether as a couple or as a whole family. It's a good time to catch up on everyone's day, to schmooze about current events, to laugh together, and to make plans for the evening or weekend. Yet consider this: one study found that two-thirds of American families do not have dinner together and half of those who do have the television on (cited in Doherty, 1999).

Other Lovers don't use these specific strategies but they make sure they are available to each other. One woman, for instance, reported that after eating dinner together, she and her husband usually go their separate ways for most of the evening: he goes downstairs to his stamp collection and she goes to her computer to work. Yet they touch base at least two times during the evening, and if one wants to talk or have some other contact, he or she has but to ask.

Not all Lovers are as fortunate regarding time. Because of their frantic work schedules, for example, one couple reported having only one day a week to be together. But they make the best of it and guard it ferociously. "I control our social calendar," reports the wife, "and although we have lots of friends we'd love to see, I limit visiting with them to no more than once a month. We both feel a little bad about this, but we have to ensure that we have enough time just for the two of us."

It's almost impossible to address the issue of time together without mentioning children because child-rearing takes so much time and energy. The Lovers with children recognized early on what a devastating effect this situation can have on marital and sexual happiness (Cowan & Cowan, 1999; Rubin, 1990; Prager, 1995) and took steps to prevent this effect on their relationships. As we will see, the Lovers made sure to have time for just the two of them even when the children were quite young. They understand that the couple and the family are separate entities and that each has to be attended to and nurtured.

I think the main point here is that Lovers don't let anything—busy schedules, monetary issues, in-laws, or young children—get in the way of putting time and energy into what is extremely important to them, their relationship.

Trust

Whether they've been together two years or 60, the Lovers have developed a profound trust in each other. They trust their partners will keep their word, will not deliberately hurt them, will see and understand their point of view even on sensitive issues, will not judge or demean them, and will usually give them what they want—in short, that their partners will be there for them—today, tomorrow, next week, next month, next year, and so on.

The drama and trauma so characteristic of unhappy relationships—the endless rounds of breaking up and making up, or the long periods of anger and distance, followed by passionate making up, soon to be followed by more anger and distance, and on and on—is nowhere in evidence in successful relationships, although they may have been in the past. Distance is rare and anger is quickly dealt with. There are no threats or hints of affairs or divorces. As one man put it, "No one's going any-where. We're here together for as long as we live and we need to make the best of what life throws our way. Looking at it this way sure helps." Another Lover said this of her partner: "He's more trusting, less defended, more present and more open than he's been in other rela-tionships and than he was in the beginning with me. He doesn't have one foot out the door; he's not tentative; he's just safely here."

Lovers trust that whatever "life throws our way" can be handled by the two of them. No matter how horren-dous—serious problems with children, illness and injury, deaths of parents and friends, financial setbacks—what-ever problems arise will be dealt with in the best manner possible and together.

Lovers have learned that they will not be punished for being themselves. They can express their ideas, feelings, dreams, fears, and anything else without worrying that they will be demeaned, judged, humiliated, or thought to be insane. This freedom translates into an extraordinary sense of safety, which in turn makes happiness easy to come by.

Because they feel they can be themselves, Lovers are usually quick to bring up complaints. If they don't like something that's going on or that their partner has done, they say so. One man in a very happy relationship said this: "We do period assessments of our relationship. We try to deal with the issues before they become big prob-lems." For some couples, as we saw with Molly and Sam in the last chapter, getting to this point took time and work. At first it was frightening to bring up complaints, even about trivial matters.

I think the main reason we rarely see happy couples in movies and plays, or read about them in novels, is precisely because of lack of drama. Although it feels terrific to be in a loving relationship and to experience peace and harmony, it doesn't make for good theater. It doesn't have the suspense—will she betray him or not? will he tell her about his affair in his first marriage? will she buy the expensive sports car without consulting him? will he stay or leave?—that are the staple of our entertainment. But watching or reading about trauma and drama is one thing, living it is something else entirely. As one of the Lovers put it: "I've had enough high drama to last several lifetimes. God spare me any more of that shit. I love the consistency and security we've achieved in our marriage."

Acceptance

Because Lovers like, respect, and understand each other, and because a tremendous amount of goodwill comes from their many positive interactions, they tend to accept one another, including the parts they don't love so much. An example of this is a husband whose second wife does not enjoy his grandson from a previous marriage (this grandson is a very difficult child). When he goes to visit the boy, or babysit for him, his wife does not usually go along. Yet there is no resentment on her part that he's taking time away from her to visit the boy, and no anger on his part that she's not participating. She understands and accepts why he has to go and he understands and accepts why she chooses not to.

Another man said of his wife, who had put on weight over the years, a quality that is not inherently appealing to him, "I know it's the same old gal I love so much underneath it all. The weight just isn't that important."

Lovers are in very close contact with reality. They know their partners far better than do those in unhappy unions. They do not have their heads in the clouds, nor are they in denial. But they focus much more on the positive and are much more accepting of their partner's shortcomings. As one man put it when discussing his partner's volatility:

> I can't have her any other way. It's just part of who she is, part of the package. And let me tell you, I love that package, so the occasional outbursts are OK with me. Well, maybe not totally OK. If I could have her without the blowups, I'd certainly welcome it. I admit that I still find them annoying. But since I can't have her any other way, I accept her as she is.

Another Lover says this: "After you've lived with someone for so long, there are things you just accept."

Another way of talking about the acceptance Lovers have for one another is to say that they have given up the fantasies that unhappy individuals and couples constantly engage in—the fantasy that the partner will change, that he or she will become neater, cleaner, more responsible, lose weight, make more money, and on and on. As one woman put it about her very unhappy first marriage:

> I knew from the start that I didn't like him as he was, but what kept me with him all those years was this crazy idea in my head that he had potential and someday would realize it. It's sad that it took so many years to realize that there is no potential, there's only what you see because that's what you get. If that's not enough, get out. Better yet, don't get in.

A crucial practical corollary of acceptance is forbearance; in other words, keeping one's mouth shut at times. Lovers don't keep harping on the behaviors and traits of their partners that they don't especially like. This practice is well described by television news analysts Cokie and Steven Roberts in their account of their 33-year marriage:

> What you don't say in a marriage can be as important as what you do say. We often joke that the success of a marriage can be measured by the number of teeth marks in your tongue. Keeping quiet in the first place means you don't have to say 'I'm sorry' quite so often." (Roberts & Roberts, 2000, p. xi)

The man who spoke of his wife's excess weight, for example, has never brought this up as an issue to her. What would be the point except to hurt her feelings? Similarly, the man who doesn't love his partner's volatility doesn't criticize her for it or even mention it.

I was reminded about forbearance or tact early in my research. I had intended to interview couples together but two women whom I contacted for interviews and who turned out to be among the Lovers urged me to interview partners separately. They both advised me that if I interviewed couples together, I wouldn't hear the whole story. For example, in one case, the man's body was badly scarred in a serious car accident, and his wife was no longer as attracted by his body as she had been. She didn't want to mention it in front of him because she knew it would hurt his feelings. In the other case, the husband had developed erection problems and his wife didn't want to mention it in front of him because she knew how distraught he was over this development. There were no secrets here, both partners knew about the scars and the erection problem, but they did not want to hurt each other. That's forbearance.

Now this definition of forbearance may seem to contradict the point I made previously about Lovers bringing up problems early on. But I don't believe it's a real contradiction. Lovers generally can discern what kinds of issues are not worth broaching because it will only cause pain and they can't be changed anyway, from what kinds of questions or feelings are worth expressing. It's a balancing act for sure, but Lovers seem better at it than other folks.

Among other things, forbearance means that the kind of carping and nagging common in so many relationships is not much in evidence. One woman stated it quite well:

> There's been an enormous change for me over time.
> I finally get it. The other is other and differences
> between myself and him are enduring. He is an adult
> who is successful and capable in his own life.
> Somehow he's managed to do what he's needed to
> do his whole life without my instruction and advice. I
> don't have to teach him about this or that. My task is
> to enjoy the ways in which he enriches my life. And
> the ways in which he doesn't, that's OK.

Many Lovers reported that earlier in their lives, without even being much aware of it at the time, they had treated their partners like children or defective adults, who didn't know how to eat, drive, dress, get organized, or talk properly. This kind of constant critiquing goes on in distressed relationships all the time. Yet the Lovers realized, some with the help of therapy, others without, that this kind of constant badgering leads only to arguments or their partner shutting down. In no way does carping and criticizing enhance relationships.

Some Lovers noted that unless the partner's behavior directly affects them and is something that can be changed, silence is the way to go. A man in his 60s:

> I'm so embarrassed at how often I used to tell my girl-
> friends how to drive—'slow down, you're going to
> miss the exit, watch out for the guy on the right, speed
> up now, damn, you missed the light because you
> were going too slow' God, it was terrible. No wonder I
> had such trouble with relationships. Praise be that I
> realized this stuff is totally uncalled for. All my girl-
> friends have been safer drivers than me, so they
> weren't endangering me. Is it really that important if

we get there five minutes later or if she drives in a different lane than I would choose? The answer, of course, is no. At first, it took constant effort not to attend to and criticize her driving. But I'm at the point now where I don't even notice how she's driving. I focus on our conversation, on the music from the radio, or on my own thoughts. And that's a big reason I'm now able to have such a good relationship.

When I asked if that meant he never brings up complaints, he responded with this:

No, that's not it. It's hard to explain. Criticizing her driving was bad simply because she wasn't doing anything wrong. She just had a different style of driving and it wasn't going to change. Actually, there was no reason it should. But there was something else that affected me more directly that I thought could change: her failure sometimes to write down work-related messages that came on the home phone. This I felt fully justified in bringing up so I had a serious talk with her about it and I also made sure there was always note paper and pens near both phones. She made a concerted effort and it worked out. She hasn't missed a message in years.

I know some readers will have trouble with the idea of forbearance because the notion has gotten around in recent years that a relationship is the perfect place to express all your feelings and let it all hang out, to be, "totally honest". As one man said, "If I can't be my real self at home and let all my feelings out, where can I?" The answer, as sad as it may seem to this man, is nowhere. The only time you can get away with expressing all your cruel, hateful, and unkind feelings is when you are two years old. The two-year-old child can yell, "I hate you, you're not my real mother, I wish you were dead", because we assume such a young child doesn't know what he or she is really saying.

But those words from an adult would hurt the other person. He or she would likely respond angrily and soon everyone would feel terrible and the relationship would be in much worse shape. Although you can certainly express your likes and dislikes, the latter has to be done with some thought and kindness. You need to protect your partner from the worst in you, otherwise the price is very high.

Total openness or honesty is a myth perpetrated by some therapists and some talk-show hosts who have no idea what they're talking about. Assuming that it was possible to be totally honest, which I doubt, the person following that practice is going to end up alone.

Mutual support

Because of their acceptance and forbearance, Lovers are in a good position to sustain and back up one another. Instead of constantly criticizing each other, as so many couples do, Lovers support each other. As a married woman with a wonderful marriage and sex life put it, "If I have a tiff with a colleague, my partner always sees it my way and is totally supportive. I always experience this unconditional positive regard from him. It's wonderful."

Another Lover offered this: "We're each other's cheerleader and primary support system."

Perhaps the primary vehicle of support is the regular giving of compliments and appreciations (or C and A, as I refer to them). Lovers are constantly expressing in private and also in front of others the good qualities of their partners. This is what John Gottman calls a culture of appreciation, as opposed to what we see in unhappy unions, a culture of criticism.

As an example, a woman in her 60s and married nine years, recounted this experience: "One morning I had to run down to the office for two hours and my husband decided to stay home and work. When I returned, he beamed when I walked in, as he always does, and said: 'I'm so glad to see you. I've missed you so much.'" She continued: "He's always saying things like that. How could I not love this man?" A man married over 30 years says:

> We tell each other every day how much we love each other. We make sure to say how good the other one looks, how thoughtful they are, and so forth. Sometimes I leave notes for her saying how beautiful or sexy she is or how lucky I am to have her.

By contrast, the unhappy couples who come to me for marital counseling rarely express positive thoughts and feelings to each other. Even when they're not busy criticizing, they don't think to express compliments. Often the partners cannot remember when they last gave or received a compliment or appreciation. I recently saw a couple in therapy, both of whom are in their late 30s. Their relationship is fairly good but not great, and one reason is the relative absence of positive expression. When I asked if they ever had positive thoughts or feelings about the other, they both immediately responded "of course". But there was silence when I asked what percentage of those feelings were expressed verbally to the partner. Finally, the woman said, "I'd say I'm in the low single digits." The man said about 30 percent. Here is a young couple who grew up during a time when all the relationship experts on television and in the newspapers and magazines were constantly telling them to communicate, and they are expressing less than a third of the positive feelings they have for each other! And they wonder why they don't feel happier. Lovers do not behave this way. When they feel something positive about the partner, which is frequently, they say so.

Clearly, men and women who feel constantly criticized do not feel good most of the time, whereas those who regularly get their share of C and A have a much happier outlook on life, and are grateful for the person who makes them feel good.

Keeping in touch

Affectionate touching is another way to express love and support, and Lovers tend to be touchers. They like to hold hands, hug and kiss, cuddle, sit close together, and so on. Karen (more about her in Chapter 11) said the following:

> " It's funny how much we like to stay in touch. When we watch a movie on TV, we're practically sitting on top of each other even though we have this huge couch. "

Another woman gave this perspective:

> " We're primates and primates spend a lot of time holding and grooming each other. We need that and when we don't get it, we get weird. My husband and I do a lot of touching, in and out of the bedroom. "

Another Lover said that he and his wife have always had a double bed even though they have a immense bedroom and could easily afford a larger bed: "What would be the point? We like to sleep right next to each other so we can feel each other. It's always been like this." And Sam, of Molly and Sam whom we learned about in the last chapter, reported that in recent years he and his wife have at least a "one minute hug upon leaving and arriving— that's important to us."

An 80-year-old woman speaks of touching in her marriage of 43 years:

> " There wasn't a day, and our children can vouch for this, that there wasn't hugs and kisses and dancing around the room. Physical affection was very important. Sometimes he'd embarrass me at the mall. "

As I listened to the recordings of my interviews with the Lovers, focusing especially on what they had to say about physical affection, I was reminded of a line in a song by Steve Winwood of some years ago, "Holding on, every day and every night." It's something Lovers believe in and put into practice far more than other couples, and it clearly makes a difference.

Dealing quickly and constructively with conflict and anger

Disagreements and conflicts exist in every relationship, as does anger, and effective means have to be found to deal with them lest they destroy everything. Some people don't understand or believe this. According to them, happy couples shouldn't have conflicts, certainly not any that are difficult or impossible to resolve. But this is fantasy. As researcher John Gottman and couple therapist Dan Wile have demonstrated, every couple has unresolved and unresolvable differences and conflicts. As Wile puts it so well: "When you start a relationship, you are in essence choosing a particular set of unresolvable problems." (Wile, 1999).

The fantasy that with the right partner we will walk into the sunset and forever enjoy peace and contentment, without clashes and arguments, is unattainable. I myself hold on to this fantasy on Valentine's Day, our anniversary, and most Mondays, Tuesdays, and Saturday evenings. At all other times, I have a tighter hold on reality.

The reason there will always be conflicts is simple. Because of our unique genetics, upbringing, and experiences, we each develop certain automatic styles, attitudes, and behaviors. Some of these are quite attractive to our mates and some annoying. But such things are not easily changed. Some can be, often with a lot of effort, but not most of them. In fact, John Gottman has data demonstrating that fully 69 percent of the problems in a relationship are not resolvable ever, regardless of what pressures, threats, and interventions are employed. Gottman has videos of couples having the exact same arguments 16 years later, which I think is very persuasive.

Some Lovers take issue with what I just said, claiming that there is little or no conflict in their unions. One woman, for instance, has been in a successful relationship for over three years, after a number of not-so-good ones, and says: "It's so easy. We haven't had a serious disagreement the whole time. I wish I knew this was possible when I was younger." Another woman says that there hasn't been a serious spat in eight years. But these two voices were the only ones in my sample who said this. Everyone else, Lover or not, said conflicts and disagreements were an integral part of their unions.

Sometimes conflicts are dealt with so smoothly and quickly that strong negative emotion doesn't have time to develop. A 78-year-old Lover insisted that he and his wife hadn't fought in years. I kept pushing him, insisting that there must be some things they didn't agree on. Finally, in desperation, I made up an example in which he wanted to spend their vacation fishing in Maine whereas she wanted to go to Paris, and then I declared that now there was a problem. "Nope," he said, "I'd give in right away. Paris is OK with me." When I questioned how he would feel always yielding to her, he said it wasn't a problem because she always gave in as well. He then said: "Young man [I liked that part], I don't think you get it. What's important to me is being with her. I don't really care if I go fishing in Maine or sightseeing in Paris. Those things are not that important."

But most Lovers say there was conflict and anger aplenty in earlier years and even now. Lovers do get irritated, frustrated, and angry with one another. Sometimes they yell. Anger, annoyance, and frustration in themselves do not indicate a bad relationship.

What differentiates Lovers from other couples is how they deal with conflict and anger. Even when they really get into it, they have rules (which can differ from couple to couple) about what is permissible and what is not. They fight fairly within their own parameters; in other words, the rules they follow are their own and not necessarily those prescribed by therapists and self-help books. They complain about behaviors and not about personalities (e.g., "I'm really pissed that you told your friend Kate about my sex problem" rather than "You're irresponsible and untrustworthy"). And they almost never bring up personal vulnerabilities and weaknesses. A Lover would never say what one woman said with contempt in my office a few weeks ago to her husband: "Let's face it. You've failed me and the children. You're a shit salesman, a complete failure, and you can't support us in a decent style. And now you want me to get a job! If you had any balls, you'd figure out something instead of turning to me." No matter how angry they are, Lovers do not go for the jugular. They know that certain words and phrases are unacceptable, as are threats of leaving the relationship.

Another characteristic that separates Lovers from unhappy couples is that they quickly repair potentially damaging interactions. Before too much time passes, they sense that what they're doing is endangering their love, so they go to work immediately to get on a different track. Some couples have rules about not going to bed angry, so they'll stay up to all hours until the negative feelings dissipate. Other couples have gone to bed angry, but they remedy things first thing in the morning. This is in contrast to what unhappy couples do, let a problem completely take over or simmer just beneath the surface of the relationship for days, weeks, or months. Here's a technique that's worked effectively for over 25 years for one couple:

> Every night before we go to sleep, no matter how we feel (and there have been a few times when one or both were very angry), we hold each other and say 'I love you'. I don't recall how or when we came up with that, but it's helped immensely over the years. It's hard to keep being pissed off when you're holding someone and hearing and saying 'I love you'.

A crucial attribute that helps, one might even say compels, Lovers to resolve conflicts as expeditiously as possible is exemplified in these two statements: "Being alienated from each other is so painful that we quickly have to work out our problems" and "I learned that being right is not as important as being together; I can't stand being disconnected from him." This fierce desire to be connected to the partner combined with an intense dislike of not having that connection, is common among the Lovers. It also leads Lovers to discover ways to reduce conflict altogether. Back to Karen for a moment. She reports finding something that helped cut down on the amount of disconnected time. Her marriage wasn't always as satisfying as it has been in recent years. One thing the couple learned was, in her words, "to cut to the chase and ask, 'Is this really that important?' If it's not, and most of the time it isn't, we back off. Because of this, we have less conflict."

A man married 45 years says that occasionally he and his wife get so riled up, he has to take a time out. After his feelings settle down, he comes back and then, "We talk it over and decide how to handle it." He describes the first year of their marriage as "very rough", but he says they did eventually learn to communicate. Things have been easier ever since. One reason is that they divided up responsibilities. "She's the boss about some things and I'm in charge of other things. Then there are things we both have to agree on and that's where being able to talk and compromise come in."

There is almost no holding of grudges and no reminding the other of something they did wrong 10 years ago, something which unhappy couples do frequently. Once Lovers resolve an issue, it tends to be over. There isn't continuous repetition of the same complaints. Once the issue is voiced and an acceptable response is given, whether an apology or a new plan for the next time, it's done. Lovers usually resist the common human impulse to make the partner wrong and to kick them when they're down. Words and touches that allow the partner to save face are more the norm.

Exactly how do these people go about handling anger in the ways I have described? Here is how one woman explains the mechanism. She told me of a recent four-day business trip she made. She and her husband spent a lot of time on the phone while she was away, with lots of expressions of love and lust. She was exhausted when she returned home in the evening but was looking forward to a loving time, including the fantasy that he would have prepared a warm dinner for her. But he hadn't. In fact, there wasn't any food in the house. Immediately, she started to feel angry, telling herself, "If you love me so much, why the hell couldn't you at least have gone shopping?" Such statements, of course, are a great way to increase and maintain anger. She described the cycle of emotion: "I was working myself into a state of indignation, which is easy for me. But I caught myself. I know him. He doesn't think to shop. It's not personal. After all, there was nothing for him to eat either. That's just who he is. And we have so much that's wonderful, I'm not willing to jeopardize it for the momentary satisfaction of feeling victimized. So I let it go." This is a marvelous example of making cognitive adjustments, of talking oneself out of destructive feelings and into more positive ones.

Other Lovers offer similar statements about telling themselves that what the other did was not aimed at them and therefore not personal, that the partner was doing his or her best, and that there is so much good in their relationship. These 'techniques' may sound simplistic and corny, especially on paper, but they work. They also form, although I doubt most of the Lovers know this, a large part of what goes on in cognitive therapy, a modern short-term psychotherapy that has proven its effectiveness in a number of scientific studies.

What these perspectives share is a tendency to hold onto some of the good feelings about the partner or the relationship even while being upset or angry. As far as I can tell, Lovers rarely or never give themselves totally over to negative emotions. Some part of them holds on to the goodness of their partner, no matter how angry they are, and this allows them to moderate their responses. Or, as one Lover expressed it: "Just because I'm angry with him doesn't mean I forget how cute he is." The Lover's ability to deal relatively easily with anger, at least compared to unhappy couples, is also bolstered by two other considerations. First, as already noted, Lovers tend to bring up complaints and annoyances fairly quickly, before they have time to fester and grow to unmanageable proportions. And second, Lovers really do have very good relationships. Most of their time together is happy, even joyful. Because of that, the bad stuff is easier to overlook or get over. It's easier to say, "Ah, who cares?" or to forgive or to make short work of something when there's a backdrop of caring, affection, and good times.

I had the impression that the Lovers had to a significant degree transcended their individual egos. The relationship loomed larger to them than their individual selves. Therefore, flexibility and compromise were comparatively easy. This is not to say that either partner sold out. Both partners were equally busy pleasing each other. When both partners feel and act this way, you see something remarkable. And for the most part these people are independent, assertive, happy, and successful in getting what they want out of life. By no means are Lovers pushovers or wimps.

Individuals in troubled relationships, on the other hand, have an excess of ego. Being right is extremely important, as if it really mattered who said what in the car or exactly what day that conversation took place. I have seen unhappy clients argue for most of a therapy session as to whether a certain event occurred on Wednesday night or Thursday, or last week or the week before. These kinds of conversations are sure signs that being right and ego rule the relationship. Lovers give in easily on these matters. They know making the partner wrong or making themselves right leads to nothing constructive.

Equanimity

Another consideration in dealing with conflict and anger that's important to mention is equanimity. Many of the behaviors of the Lovers are supported by an underlying attitude of equanimity or tranquility. It helps tremendously if at least one of the partners is *relatively* calm and able to not take things personally or when both partners manifest these tendencies at times.

A woman in her early 60s and in her second marriage, one of the very best I've ever encountered, told me a story that I think says it all on this point: It happened on an early date with her current husband. She was having one of those terrible days where nothing was going right. Everything was taking longer than expected and everything she was waiting for arrived late or not at all. Her date was for 8 p.m., and she was frantically running around trying to get ready. At 7:30 p.m., when she was nowhere near ready, the doorbell rang. She answered the door and was shocked to see that it was him. (Before you get mad at him, let me explain that he had to travel 20 miles of one of New York's most congested roads to get to her, so he allowed extra time. On this day, as luck would have it, there was little traffic.)

> I completely lost it. I thought I'd be lucky to be ready by 8:30 and here he is, half an hour early. I started shrieking: 'When I said 8, I meant 8, not 7:30, not even 7:45 or 7:55. You don't listen to me, you don't respect me, you only care about yourself.' I knew I was acting like a crazy person but I couldn't stop myself. All my frustrations came pouring out. But he didn't get caught up in it. When I finally stopped to catch my breath, he simply smiled and said: 'I think this would be a good time for me to take a walk. Why don't I come back in an hour or so?' If he had gotten defensive or told me off, which would have been richly deserved, I would have gotten even crazier. But his calm broke it for me. I apologized for my behavior and invited him to come in and have a glass of wine while

I got myself organized. His calm calmed me. I'm a lucky woman because he's almost always like this. The shit in life, including my shit, doesn't really get to him.

Any relationship benefits to the extent that one or both of the partners can manifest this demeanor or when both partners manifest it some of the time. What's dangerous is when one partner's anger triggers the other's anger and there's a downward spiral of ever-increasing anger, because this means no one is calm or reasonable, no one can self-soothe or console the other, and the result is that all rules are forgotten, love and appreciation are forgotten, and horrible things get said and done, which usually cannot be forgotten, and everything goes to hell.

When there are two partners together who don't usually take things personally, who don't have to win, and who at least can take turns remaining relatively calm and mindful when the other one is falling apart or expressing frustration, irritation, or anger, then you have something close to perfection.

Chapter 8

Intention

We have already noted that while a caring, stable relationship is necessary for good lovemaking over time, it is not sufficient. More is needed.

The Lovers have in common an intention to have and maintain a good sex life. It is probably the case that because lust is a large component of initial attraction and because sexual frequency tends to be high in the early stages of a relationship, new couples simply assume it will continue at the same rate and quality. Many even believe their sex lives will improve after marriage. If there's a glitch, time will fix it. But that's a strange notion since time is neutral; time doesn't *do* anything. Things may get better with time, or they may get worse; it's also possible that the passage of time will have no effect on the matter at all. But getting back to our main point, assuming and intending are not the same: the former is passive, the latter active.

Lovers may or may not assume, but what's important is that they intend. Sex is a high priority to them and they expect to work at it to make sure it's a regular and fun part of their lives. Regarding its importance, a woman put it simply: "It's *the* glue that keeps a loving relationship together." Regarding intention, a man had this to say: "This being a second marriage for both of us, we knew from experience what can happen to sex after the honeymoon. We decided we didn't want that to happen again to us and we vowed that we would do everything in our power to become dirty old people together. We wanted to be an embarrassment to our children and, by God, we've succeeded."

To put the matter of intention another way, Lovers choose to make sex a priority and have great sex lives. This reminds me of what Rick Foster and Greg Hicks found in their study of happiness, *How We Choose to be Happy* (1999). The happy people in their research actually chose and intended, consciously and deliberately, to be happy. It was not something that just happened. They daily set out to be happy and took the necessary steps to reach that state of mind. When I first read this, I had a hard time believing it. Come on, I thought, people actually sitting on their beds or looking in the mirror while brushing their teeth and planning how to be happy that day. No way. Real people don't act like that. I may impulsively jump to conclusions at times, but I am smart enough to know that this tendency needs constant checking. So the next time I met with a woman friend who is one of the most together and happy people I know, I asked her what she thought of Foster and Hicks' conclusion. Much to my surprise, she said she understood it perfectly. She herself did it every morning.

At this point, some readers may object that intention should not be necessary when sex is such a powerful drive. Although I understand the logic, it is simply not true. Sex is one of the first things to go in a relationship. The couple that couldn't keep their hands off each other in their third month of courtship may suddenly realize, now that they have been living together for two years, that they haven't made love in three months. After interviewing nearly 1,000 men and women, Lillian Rubin found the following: "Sexual interest and activity are at their height during dating and courtship, take a drop when people begin to live together, then another fall after marriage, and show the most precipitous decline after the first child is born." (1990, p. 163) And her sample consisted entirely of people under the age of 48! She is not even talking about the old folks.

Despite all the news about erection difficulties and other so-called dysfunctions, lack of sexual interest and activity have been the main problems brought to sex therapists for the last 20 years. We are faced daily in our practices with couples who haven't had sex in months, years and—I know this will be hard for some to believe—even in decades. In what is considered to be the best sex survey ever conducted, 33 percent of the women said they were uninterested in sex as did 15 percent of the men (Michael *et al*, 1994, p. 126). These figures do not include those who say they are interested, but are so busy, hassled, and tired that it just doesn't happen very often.

In an ongoing relationship there are so many demands, pressures, and things to attend to that sex can easily get lost. Rubin (1990) says it well:

> On the most mundane level, the constant negotiation about everyday tasks leaves people harassed, weary, irritated and feeling more like traffic cops than lovers. Who's going to do the shopping, pay the bills, take care of the laundry, wash the dishes, take out the garbage, clean the bathroom, get the washing machine fixed, decide what to eat for dinner, return the phone calls from friends and parents? When there are children, the demands, complications and exhaustion increase exponentially (p. 165).

Of course, couples at midlife and beyond generally don't have children, or at least not young children, to care for. But neither do they have the hormonal gushes and physical energy they had when they were younger; instead of children to deal with, they may have their own parents needing regular care or even living with them.

Sex is important to Lovers. They are mindful of how often they make love and how good it is. They monitor it and don't take good sex for granted. They seem to know they are going to work at it, that they can't just assume sex will take care of itself. "We've made it a priority", "We put it ahead of other things", "We always made time for it", "We always made sure to make a place for it", were statements I frequently heard from the Lovers.

In the next chapter, I show how Lovers take responsibility for having great sex and don't let obstacles get in the way. But to demonstrate here how intention plays out, I take up the question of how Lovers keep their sexuality intact when they have young children in the house. At this point you may be wondering why I spend so much time here and elsewhere on what Lovers do regarding having children, especially young children, in the home. After all, most couples over the age of 45 don't have infants crawling around demanding attention. That's true, but most of the Lovers had young children around at some earlier point in their lives together and dealing with that situation creatively and successfully is what allowed many of them to develop and maintain the positive sexual interactions that are such an important part of their lives today. I do not want to give the impression that if you let the children interfere or even completely disrupt your romance 10, 20, or 30 years ago, you can't relight the fire now. Of course you can. However, it's instructive to look at what some of the Lovers did earlier in their lives.

It is well known that the arrival of the first child is enough to put a dent in any couple's sex life. The more children the greater the potential damage. Many couple's erotic lives do not recover until the last child leaves home, if even then. While there is no question that infants and children are extremely demanding and can sap the energy of even Olympic athletes, there is also no question that lots of parents use the children as a convenient excuse not to have sex.

I know of no evidence that Lovers neglect their children. But they are aware that the adult relationship, both generally and sexually, must be maintained even with children in the home. Put differently, they know the family is not the same as the couple. It's not always easy, but they work at it. They squeeze in a quickie when the child is down for a nap. They arrange babysitting and go out for evening or overnight trips, just the two of them, even when the children are young. Because they intend to keep eroticism alive and because they take responsibility for making it happen, they do not allow sex to wither on the vine.

Jessica offers a powerful example of how far a Lover is willing to go to keep love alive. She and Bo had an impressive sex life for the first 10 years.

> It was better than either of us had experienced before and better than we ever expected to have. Sex was at the core of our relationship and we vowed we would keep making sweaty, noisy love until we died. And then, much to our surprise, we decided to have a child. As a result, we almost lost our sexuality.

She continued:

> Having a child at any age is exhausting, but I was old—41 to be exact—and I was tired all the time. It didn't help that our first child was colicky and Bo couldn't help at night. I had stopped working so he was the only one bringing in money, and he had to be able to perform at work during the day. It was all up to me with the baby and I was too pooped to pop. We just stopped having sex. Well, not entirely, because a few months after the first child, I found myself pregnant again. This we hadn't planned on. With two

infants, it was even worse. One day I realized that we hadn't made love in five months. It scared the day-lights out of me. I panicked as I imagined the future. We were going to be like all the other couples. We were losing our steamy, bonding, ecstatic love life. I couldn't stand the idea.

As tired as I was, I talked to Bo that night. We agreed we couldn't go on this way. I seduced him right there. I could hardly keep my eyes open, but I insisted he fuck me. When it was over, I told him I wanted to make love at least once a week. When he countered that I always looked so tired, I told him to make an advance whenever he felt like it and, no matter how I responded, to take me anyway. He said that sounded like rape and he couldn't do it. My retort was that it couldn't be rape since I was the one making the sug-gestion. I went so far as to demand that if he wanted me when I was sleeping, he should apply lube and go right ahead.

Sounds crass when I describe it, but it worked. Usually, of course, I got turned on as soon as the action started and had a good time. We were both happy to be back on track. As the boys got older, we headed back to our pre-baby frequency.

Now, years later, the boys are in college and Jessica and Bo are happy as clams, still having sex two to three times a week. "I know we did the right thing," Jessica reports.

Most of the couples our age that we know don't have sex or not much. We're the big-time lovers in our social circle. I'm proud of us. I think where we are today is a direct result of us not letting the babies rob us of our love life.

Other couples provide similar, though perhaps less dramatic stories. Many of them talk about getting babysitters even when the children were quite young so they could have dates, sometimes at nearby motels. Some went for overnight getaways. Recall that Betsy and Wade realized early on that it was essential for their "couple-ness" that they spend time away from their two young girls. One woman realized she was, for the first time ever, very quiet during sex because the baby slept in an alcove in their bedroom. As soon as the child was old enough, she was moved to a separate room. Another woman said that as soon as their child was old enough, he was moved to a different floor of the house.

It's not just young children who can negatively affect a couple's sex life. Some parents allow teenage and even grown-up children to put a crimp in their sexuality. They won't make love, for instance, if the children are still awake or if the children have friends stay over night. Lovers, of course, do things differently. They don't let children of any age, or almost anything else, interfere with their romantic interludes. They put on music to mask their noises if that's a problem, or they make less noise, move to a different room further away, or put the children in one. One way or another, they make sure they have the freedom to make love.

Regularity

An important aspect of intention is regularity. Lovers have sex on a regular basis.

In many areas of life, regularity is important. If you hadn't brushed your teeth for many months, or weren't brought up to brush your teeth, it would be difficult to start the routine of brushing twice every day. In the beginning, there would be many times when you would simply forget. Or you would remember after you were already on the way to work or in bed and wouldn't want to take the trouble to brush. Yet once you get into the routine of brushing as soon as you wake up and before getting into bed, it's easy. The habit is established, you just brush.

Although there are many differences between making love and brushing teeth, the routine part is similar. Many of my clients, and most Non-lovers, don't have regular sex. There is no established practice of having sex at least once a week, or on a certain day, with the result that sex is infrequent. Non-lovers may go weeks or even months with no sex at all. And this often creates problems because when it's been that long, a tension builds up around the topic and it's difficult to get sex started again. When it's infrequent, the partners feel self-conscious and awkward, and each encounter assumes a huge importance, whereas when it's more frequent, each event is just another event; if it's not the greatest, well, there's always another chance tomorrow, in a few days, or a week or so. But if this one is it for the month or for who knows how long, too much importance is attached to it and there are questions on the part of one or both partners about how this encounter is going to go, about why it's been so long since the last one, and about how long it will be until the next one. Talk about creating or increasing performance anxiety! This atmosphere is not conducive to good sex; quite the contrary, such ruminations often result in avoidance of sex. At some point, sex may all but disappear. Sex therapists and marriage counselors will easily recognize this pattern.

Lovers maintain some kind of consistent sex life. By this I do not mean to say that all of them have sex every Wednesday at 7 a.m. or 5 p.m. Rather, the idea is that they don't go for long periods without sex. A momentum is built up and awkwardness and tension are not allowed to develop. The Lovers I interviewed varied greatly in how often they had sex, everything from two to three times a month to daily, but whatever the particular regimen, they pretty much stick to it. The only exception I found to this rule among the Lovers were people like Pearl and Karen (Chapter 10) with very serious health problems. There are times that their health is so bad, they have little energy and they may go for weeks without sex.

Many Lovers report feeling that something is missing if they haven't had sex within, say, a week. They feel restless and maybe irritable. But they know what these feelings mean and move as quickly as possible to remedy the situation—by making love.

Scheduling sex

One way of implementing intention and maintaining regularity is by scheduling sex. Many Lovers report having a regular date night during the week, just the two of them doing something fun and often having sex as well. Other Lovers say that when one of them wants sex and the other isn't in the mood, they schedule a time for lovemaking in the next day or so. As a Lover in her 80s reported:

> Sometimes when he approaches me, I'm just too tired. I know it wouldn't be good for either of us. So I suggest we make love when we wake up, or later that day or the next day. And we always do. We both get what we want and we keep our wonderful sex life going.

Another woman, this one more than 70 years old and married over 50 years:

> We make dates with each other for sex, which could be at any time. Sometimes we have it so that we'll come to bed in the middle of the day with the shades drawn, the phone answering machine on, and the doors locked, and have a lovely day.

Non-lovers often vehemently argue against the scheduling of sex. As one of them put it:

> I'll be damned if I want to schedule something as natural as sex. Sex should be spontaneous. Scheduling kills spontaneity and takes away the naturalness. It

> makes it into something ... I don't know, like mechanical or clinical.

Maybe, but it's interesting that those who schedule sex tend to have sex, whereas many who refuse to schedule sex end up with little or none of it.

Not every Lover couple schedules lovemaking. But one way or the other, with or without scheduling, they do make time and energy for sex, and one way or the other, they do have sex on some kind of regular basis.

Here is how Emma handles it when her husband is turned on and she isn't:

> We don't let that fly by, we take care of it. I make love to him even though I'm not in the mood, and in a very loving way. I know some feminists would say I'm selling myself out, but I can't even relate to that kind of attitude. I want to take care of his need at that time and I do it happily and tenderly. And he of course has done the same for me. To me this isn't selling yourself out, it's only a matter of doing what's necessary to maintain a strong, loving relationship over the years.

Taking time

It should be clear by now that Lovers regularly make time for lovemaking. Now here's another aspect of time that Lovers agree contributes to a good sex life: they spend a lot of time making love. As one put it: "We give ourselves lots of time. We play around, we talk to each other. We're not in a rush to get to other things."

This is not to say that Lovers never have 'quickies'. Most of them do, or did when they were younger. And many of them mentioned that they know how to make good use of a few minutes if they're aroused but need to be somewhere soon. However, given the choice, they like to take their time.

The duration of lovemaking is hardly ever talked about when comparing sexual frequency among younger and older folks, but it may deserve reflection. Say a couple in their 20s has sex five times a week on average, each encounter lasting on average 20 minutes from start to finish. That's a total of 100 minutes per week making love. Now consider a couple in their 60s who have sex only twice a week, but each occasion lasts on average about an hour. Although the younger folks are having sex more often, the older couple is actually spending more time having sex. If it looks like I'm biasing my argument by suggesting an unrealistically long duration for the older couple, you should know that a number of Lovers said they usually spend an hour or more making love. As one woman says: "I had sex more often when I was younger but spent much less time with it, 15 or 20 minutes or so. Now we take a lot more time, which makes it a lot better." What are the consequences of spending a long time making love, other than perhaps not having it as frequently? A woman in her late 50s, who has been in the current relationship for 16 years, offers:

> My orgasms keep getting better and better. This may be due to the fact that we spend so much time making love and a long time staying close to orgasm, so we're at a high level of arousal for a long time, so my orgasms tend to be more intense.

Another woman tells this story:

> With my ex, sex was perfunctory and not much fun. He wasn't into much foreplay. Since then, sex has become a lot better for me because I've been with men who really enjoyed it, enjoyed foreplay, and enjoyed pleasing me. With Jack [her lover of five years], we almost always take a lot of time. Lots of touching, talking, fondling. The more time we spend, the more aroused I get and the more orgasms I have. Sex is the best it's ever been.

And a man:

> I was much more self-centered in sex years ago. All I wanted was my orgasm and the sooner we got there, the better. That's changed. In recent years I want to enjoy the whole menu—the looking, touching, talking, and then the more intimate caressing and fondling—and make sure Jill gets as much pleasure as she can take. So we're spending much more time making love and it's fantastic.

Suggestions

We have been talking so much about others, what about you, the reader? Here are a couple of ideas to start you on your way to a better sex life.

 If you're like most couples, you and your partner have at times expressed wishes and made promises about sex to one another; e.g., to have sex more often, to do it earlier in the evening, to take more time making love, or to try locations other than the bed. Look at the wishes and promises that have not been fulfilled. Come on, it's probably most of them. Choose one of them—say, to start lovemaking earlier in the evening—and do what's necessary to actually do it sometime in the next four days.

And if you want to get to sex earlier, one possibility is to have sex before dinner. Each of you should have a snack—say, an apple or a piece of cheese—then repair to the bedroom. Have a good time first, and then ask what's for dinner. Another increasingly popular option is that one of you bring home a take-out meal. This means no cooking and no cleaning up. With a little imagination, you can probably come up with other possibilities.

 Do you and your mate usually schedule sex? If not, consider it. Suggest to your partner that since you both get home early on Wednesdays, you make a plan for next Wednesday: a nice take-out dinner to be followed by fun and games in bed. If the date goes well, consider making Wednesday evenings your regular sex night. If it doesn't go well, discuss how to make it better. Whatever option you choose, implement it as soon as possible.

Chapter 9

Problem-solving

In the last chapter I suggested that compared to other couples, Lovers have strong intentions of maintaining an active and satisfying sex life. But to be successful, intention alone is not enough. Intention in itself is an empty wish, like New Year's resolutions, and we all know what usually happens to them. Most resolutions are soon forgotten or are not kept for long. But some people are successful in implementing and maintaining resolutions. In general, it seems that Lovers are successful. They do exercise three times each week no matter what the weather or how they feel on exercise days; they do come home earlier from work on the agreed upon night; they do initiate sex more often; they do spend more time in affectionate and sensual touch.

Perhaps the main requirement for carrying out the intentions is effectively dealing with obstacles that come up. As the bumper sticker says, "Shit happens". There are myriad barriers and stumbling blocks that get in the way of keeping a relationship, including sex, fresh, and vital. These are the everyday hassles that most every couple deals with—setting up and maintaining a household; dividing the time between work and other duties and relationship upkeep; paying bills; doing chores; shopping; dealing with relatives and friends; and so forth. Those who have children or are caring for one or more of their own parents, of course, have another huge set of tasks. Dealing effectively makes all the difference to a good sex life.

To accomplish this, at least two sets of skills are necessary. The first is the ability to recognize that a situation needs help. This may sound so simple-minded as not to be worthy of mention, but as we shall soon see, many people do not recognize problems as such, or do not recognize them in a way that makes a solution possible. The second required skill is the ability to quickly and easily get into a problem-solving mode. This may also sound obvious, but we will see that many people quickly and easily get into a different frame of mind altogether and therefore delay resolution or actually make it impossible.

Recognizing problems for what they are

Recently a woman in my office complained that her husband did not do anywhere near his share of the household chores, a very common complaint of women these days, and she listed a number of things he did not do—pick up clothing and other articles from the floor; feed and walk their two dogs; food shop; laundry; and so forth. I asked the man what went through his mind when he noticed the hamper was full of dirty clothes or that there was no more milk in the refrigerator. He thought for a while and then spoke: "I hardly even notice and what I see doesn't really register inside. I guess the truth is that the lack of milk and full hamper don't mean much to me." You can call him absent-minded, unconscious, or a typical man, but no matter what you call him, the fact is that he was not seeing that there was a problem. If he doesn't recognize his behavior is an issue, then there's nothing to resolve and thus a solution is not possible. Nothing broken, nothing to fix. During our session, however, he was impressed by the depth of his wife's anger about the situation and from then on his perception was different. Only then did a solution become possible.

This man is not alone in his lack of perception or misperception. Sometimes one partner sees a problem where the other doesn't; sometimes neither partner defines the issue as a problem. In another therapy case, the woman complained that the man didn't shave or shower every day. She didn't want to be physically close to him under those circumstances. However, the man did not consider not shaving and not showering to be a problem. He saw them as "little luxuries", things he didn't have to bother doing every single day. Why he didn't figure out on his own that his odor and bristly face might be turn-offs to his wife is another question altogether, but my point here is simply that he didn't perceive or label as a problem things that clearly were for her.

In many couples, the everyday kinds of predicaments are not seen in a way that fosters resolution. The proper way to frame such a situation, I believe, would be to see it as something that's important, something that is having a negative effect on their lives, and something, whether caused by them or not, that needs attention soon so that it can be corrected or at least ameliorated by them. But many people do not go this way. Many allow the tasks of life and family to overwhelm the relationship, while they conduct their lives in such a way that they are so busy and tired from work, chores, and children, that they don't have enough time and energy to put into their own union. Brandon, a 60-year-old businessman, offers a good example of this position:

"We know we need to put more time into us. We've known it for years. But circumstances aren't conducive to this. The whole summer has been a disaster. My mother came for two weeks and actually stayed for three. Then her mother came for a week. The kids were there the whole time, coming and going as usual, with each trip requiring taxi service. There was also the turmoil surrounding the kitchen remodel, with workmen in the house from 8:00 to 5:00 every day and a mess full time for over two months. I'll tell you, God is not helping us find time for romance."

What Brandon doesn't see is that circumstances and God have nothing to do with the situation. He and his wife are not handling the ordinary vicissitudes of life. They are not viewing these as obstacles they can fix. Instead, they are pointing fingers at God. Put another way, they are not taking responsibility for their sexual relationship or for their relationship in general.

This perspective stops Brandon from seeing the options that are available. He doesn't, for instance, own up to the fact that the house belongs to him and his wife. They could have chosen to limit the length of their mothers' visits, or told one of them that this summer was not a good time to visit; they could have put up their guests in nearby motels. During the visits, the couple could have asked the visiting mother to take the children to the movies or the mall thus allowing grandmother and grandkids time together and themselves time alone. They also could have found something for the kids to do that didn't require chauffeuring them around. If the house was a mess because of the kitchen remodeling, they could have gone off to a motel on some nights and had the kids spend the night at friends' houses. There were many workable options but Brandon and his wife were not defining the situation in a way that would allow them to consider and adopt any of them.

Similarly, Lois refuses to see that the lack of a decent sex life with her partner is a situation created by them and therefore relatively easy to resolve. She and her husband run their house like a hotel, with visitors constantly coming and going. They're both from the midwest and have made it clear to everyone they know in that part of the country that they're always welcome at their house when they visit Seattle. Not only do relatives and friends take them up on their offer, but so do relatives and friends of relatives and friends. They have people staying at their house whom they know only casually. The couple haven't had sex in several years and they complained about it to me. When I asked why they thought that was the case, they both argued that "there just aren't enough hours in the day. Between commuting and work and the kids [both of whom had graduated from college and were still living at home] and the company, there's always too much to do." The many effective solutions that could remedy the problem are obscured by the way in which both partners view the situation.

Another crucial aspect of seeing the problem as a problem is understanding what an appropriate and effective solution looks like. For example, in Chapter 5 we read that both Jesse and Tina resorted to affairs to get what they wanted (to no avail) instead of working on the issues with their partners. It is rare for an affair with someone else to be an effective solution for a relationship problem. In fact, in most cases affairs create more problems than they solve, sometimes even destroying forever the primary relationship. The best solutions are the ones arrived at with the person you're having the problem with, your partner.

Complaining to relatives, friends, and even therapists about the problem is not an effective and appropriate solution either. It is fine to talk with a trusted friend to get support, clarification or suggestions, so long as this is accompanied by working with your partner to actually resolve the problem. Nothing can substitute for that.

The futility of these approaches reminds me of the old joke about the drunk who's looking for his lost keys under the street light because the light is better there even though that is not where he lost the keys. Seeking attention, comfort, sex, or love from people outside the relationship may be convenient and a lot easier than confronting and dealing with one's partner, but such a strategy usually does little or nothing to resolve problems within the relationship. Of course the lighting is better under the street lamp, but the keys will never ever be found there. Lovers know by instinct or experience the difference between a convenient approach and an effective one, which may help explain why so few of them have affairs and why so few of them spend much time blaming and accusing. They recognize a problem when they run into one. They also know what a good solution looks like and what to do to adopt one.

Blaming and complaining

The major obstacles to properly defining a problem as such and getting into a problem-solving mode are finger-pointing and whining. Both Brandon and Lois blamed factors outside of themselves, and, as a result, were less able to discover what they could do.

In my office I see couples blaming one another and everything and everyone else for their situation. "You're the one who's never interested", "You're the one who works 70 hours a week", "You were the one who wanted dogs and now you want me to take care of them", "You're just like your mother and I refuse to put up with it", "I never wanted this kind of marriage, I wanted something more romantic, sexier, more connected, and all I have is shit", "I'm not going to go on with this, I won't spend the

rest of my life in a loveless marriage, I'd rather be alone",
and so forth.

Some people work hard to avoid problem solving.
They'd rather moan, lament, complain, and blame everything and everyone for weeks, months, or forever. They
seem to get so much satisfaction from their negativity—
which they engage in consistently and vehemently—one
wonders if they even want to resolve the issue.

The effects of spending so much time and energy on
blaming and complaining are not surprising: an incredible waste of time, increased distance and upset, putting
off for weeks, months, or years actually dealing with the
problem, thereby making it more difficult to resolve.

Lovers are different. They know that they are responsible for their lives. There's no point blaming circumstances, someone's mother, the kids, or anything or
anyone else. They accept that they have to deal with the
cards they're dealt, and they recognize that almost any
situation can be improved if not completely fixed.

Now don't get nervous. Remember, Lovers are not perfect in this or any other regard. In the next chapter, we
meet Frank, someone who did not quickly get into a
problem-solving mode when he developed a problem
with his sexuality, an area of strength for him. He spent
several months withdrawing, blaming the surgeon, blaming God, and blaming everything else he could think of.

In this case, there really was someone at fault. Frank
had been unwilling to have a meaningful conversation
about the problem with his wife Carla and just as

unwilling to take any action to solve it. When he did come around, he acknowledged it had been his doing. He knew it, Carla knew it, and so would anyone familiar with their story. Carla's response was interesting. She could, of course, have used his behavior as a reason for behaving in kind, venting her anger, withdrawing and refusing to deal with the sexual issues, guilt-tripping him, making him pay in some way for his actions, or rather, lack of action. But she was too smart for these kinds of behaviors. She was centered in herself and knew what she wanted most of all was to reestablish the "sweet closeness" of their relationship and their ecstatic sex life. So she told him once about her frustration during the preceding months and how much she had missed him. And that was it. She then expressed her delight at his "coming home" and they went to work straightening out their situation.

Problem-solving mode

The second aspect to successfully dealing with obstacles is getting into a problem-solving mode or attitude. This means no whining at all or at least making quick work of it so you get to a place like this: "There's a problem we want to correct [specific definition of the issue]. Method A [which can be almost anything at all from having sex at a different time or in a different place than usual; using pillows to make someone more comfortable; doing different kinds of stimulation; taking or discontinuing a medicine; and even having surgery] seems to offer the best cost-benefit ratio so let's give it a try. If it doesn't work out, we can try something else." No accusations, no blame, no finger-pointing, no guilt-tripping, no recriminations. And certainly no giving up on sex. This is the way Lovers tend to do things.

Lovers see problems not as implacable enemies but just as an inevitable part of life, as things that need to be worked with and around. For Lovers, almost nothing is a reason not to have sex. There's always a way. In an earlier chapter, we saw how Lovers dealt with having young children in the house. Here are three examples of how they deal with other obstacles to good sex:

> Our parents' visits have always put a bit of a crimp in our intimate carryings on. No matter how liberated I said I was, I'm not going to fuck in the living room knowing his mother, or mine, might walk in on her way to the kitchen. We are both concerned about our parents hearing our lovemaking. We don't not make love, we just don't have intercourse if we're in the living room, we do other things, we are quieter and sometimes that's a lot of fun. We keep telling each other to stifle our noises and several times one of us has put a pillow over the other's mouth to keep the sounds down.

> Having his mom living with us meant a real lack of privacy. Our place is so small that we couldn't imagine having sex with her in the house. It took us a week to come up with a solution. We found a woman who lives not too far away who is willing for a fee, of course, to come over twice a week and take my mother-in-law out in the wheelchair for an hour and a half. We make good use of that time. She complained like crazy at

first that she didn't want to go out, especially with a stranger. But we held firm. We told her it was that or a nursing home. She straightened out real fast after that. I think she's even gotten to the place where she enjoys these outings.

The house was a mess for weeks when we put on the new roof. Not only that, even though it was spring, it was freezing inside at night. This was not good, but we came up with a reasonable, though not ideal, solution. We took over the bedroom in the back of the house that had belonged to our eldest before she left for college. It was the warmest room and the one least affected by the work. For almost a month, it became our bedroom and our make love room. The kids made fun of us for sleeping in that small room, but it served our purposes.

Handling obstacles means understanding that one has choices. You can spend Saturday morning, or a portion of it, making love, or you can spend that time raking leaves, shopping, surfing the Internet, having coffee with friends, playing softball, paying bills, or sleeping. None of these options is a necessity. They are all choices. Realizing this helps Lovers accept responsibility for the choices they make. They do not do what the couple in the next excerpt did. They were in therapy with me because of the lack of sex in their relationship. My questions are in brackets.

"We didn't get around to making love this week." [What happened?] "During the week we were both so tired from work that there was no interest." [What about the weekend?] "We thought we would get together

Saturday but we had lots of shopping to do and that's what we did. When we were done, we were pooped and fell asleep." [What kind of shopping?] "First we went to the market to do our weekly grocery shopping. Then we drove to a different mall to get food for the dog." [Why not get the dog food at the grocery store?] "Well, the dog likes this special food you can get only at this one pet store." [Were you totally out of people food or dog food?] "Not really, but we were low on a few items and we like a fully stocked larder. Then we spent several hours looking for a new computer." [What did you buy?] "We didn't. We aren't going to buy for several months. We just wanted to see what was available." [Was any of the shopping or looking you did necessary?] "Well, not in that sense, but it's just stuff we felt we had to do. I know it sounds like we're making excuses, but you have to understand there's just so much to do and too little time."

This couple chose to spend their time shopping for items that were not necessary. There was no urgency about anything they shopped for, as they readily admitted. They simply chose to do these things rather than to spend time together and make love. If that's how they want to live, it's fine with me. But they refuse to see it this way. According to them, they would really like to make love they just can't find the time. In other words they refuse to recognize their responsibility for not choosing lovemaking over other options.

Another aspect of problem-solving is getting appropriate outside help if that is required. For relationship predicaments, we have therapists, and for sex problems, we have therapists and medical doctors. I regret that I didn't have a question about the use of these resources in my interview schedule. Because of this omission, I am unable to compare the use of such resources among Lovers and others. What I can say, however, is that a number of Lovers mentioned deriving benefits from medical or therapeutic consultation. Among these are Karen and Paul (Chapter 10) during a rough period in their marriage several years ago, and Ben and Holly (Chapter 6) who give an enormous amount of credit to psychotherapy for helping them build their fantastic relationship and sexuality. Just another illustration of how Lovers are willing to do whatever is necessary to resolve their difficulties.

Earlier I recounted how Lois and her partner blamed their lack of sex on the constant overnight visitors they had at their house. And one can certainly make a strong case that running one's life like this will be a deterrent to good sex. But the truth is it's just another excuse. If it isn't immediately apparent, the couple or individual who doesn't actually want sex will find a reason somewhere. After all some Lovers have frequent guests and they still manage to have active sex lives.

Samantha and Vic are one such couple. They both have several children from previous marriages who come to visit for a night or a week, often bringing a girlfriend or boyfriend along. Samantha has more best friends than anyone on the planet and these people are often there to spend their vacations. There are also other visitors. Samantha and Vic like the company, although they also like complaining about it, and they are also Lovers. They do not let these people get in their way. They feel free to announce to their company at a certain point in the evening that they (the company) should feel free to do whatever they want and stay up as late as they like, but their hosts (Samantha and Vic) are going to bed. They feel free to tell the company that they might enjoy going to eat at a certain place or seeing a certain sight, but they (Samantha and Vic) need to have some time alone. When your intention is strong and clear, and you're willing to recognize and deal with barriers to your goal, you usually get what you want.

Flexibility

I've noted a number of times that the lives of the Lovers are not necessarily ideal. They have the same problems with careers and jobs, money, in-laws, and children that everyone else has. They also have their share of illnesses, disabilities, physical discomforts, and sexual difficulties. They just don't let these things interfere with what is important to them.

In order to implement their intention to have good sex, Lovers are flexible. Instead of ranting and whining that all they got was lemons, they make lemonade, and a very fine brew at that. In other words, they are open to possibilities and options. They make the best of what life offers them.

On the other hand, a number of people I interviewed, as well as a great many clients over the years, who don't have good sex said they gave up on sex because of _____ (fill in the blank). One of the most common reasons was that the man wasn't having erections or reliable erections. Another reason was various health problems. Yet another reason was that the woman had gained weight and the man had therefore lost interest. All of these are simply a part of life.

Some people are adamant that sex has to be a certain way. The partners must conform to a certain standard of weight and beauty, the man must have a long-lasting and firm erection, only this or that partner can initiate, only this or that can be said or done, and sex can only take place at certain times and under certain conditions. These people are not flexible. If they don't get exactly what they want when they want it, they'd rather sulk and have nothing than make the best of what they have. These people are not Lovers.

And sometimes what they do is much worse than sulking. The most dramatic example I have in this regard involved an extremely demanding woman who became so upset when her 64-year-old partner lost his erection in their hotel room one night that she had a screaming fit lasting for over 15 minutes during which she threw ashtrays, baggage, and the telephone against the wall. People in adjoining rooms assumed that she was being abused and called hotel security. Within minutes, the naked man, feeling humiliated while trying to get his partner to calm down as she screamed what a rotten lover he was and continued to throw things, was faced with security knocking at the door demanding he open it immediately and threatening to use their own key if he didn't. Interestingly, neither the man nor his partner had any idea what was causing his erection problem and his lack of interest in sex.

In another case, the wife routinely responded to her husband's lack of response to her stimulation of his penis with well-chosen phrases such as "I want a hard-on, not some little squishy thing." In yet another sex therapy case, the husband of a woman who had difficulty having orgasms frequently called her frigid and, when stimulating her, made comments such as "How long is this going to take? I'm getting tired" and "This sure isn't my idea of fun."

Lovers, as they themselves say, respect one another and take good care of each other. They do not dismiss, demean, or abuse their partners. They do recognize and acknowledge problems, probably much quicker than other folks, but they find ways around them.

Of the Lovers I interviewed, a number have sexual difficulties of one kind or another. The most common for the men is erection problems and a number of solutions have been adopted. A few couples have given up on erections and intercourse, and instead rely on oral and manual stimulation, some men are using penile injections, a number are on Viagra, and a few have penile implants. The women generally have fewer serious problems than the men but there are those who mentioned desire and arousal problems. A number are on hormone replacement therapy, mainly estrogen but some on testosterone. Insufficient lubrication is a common condition among the women Lovers but they don't see it as a major problem, and neither do their partners, but rather as a minor issue that in most cases is easily remedied by using artificial lubricants.

There's nothing unique or interesting about these solutions, all of which are widely available. What struck me, however, is how little drama was involved in adopting and using them. In one case, for instance, the man lost a good deal of sensitivity in his penis due to many years of being diabetic and probably also due to recent prostate surgery. He discovered he could still have erections and orgasms, but only if his partner supplemented her stroking of him with sexy words and stories. Although this couple had never before used this kind of stimulation, once they recognized what was required, they adopted it. The change wasn't necessarily easy. The woman had no experience recounting her erotic fantasies and making up juicy sexual stories, so she bought and looked through a few books of erotica to get a better understanding of what was required. According to her partner, she learned quickly and well; he describes her as having "a PhD in using dirty words and creating arousing stories and fantasies".

Contrast that report with this therapy case. The man had trouble reaching orgasm without anal stimulation. But his wife absolutely refused to put her finger in his anus during sex. Not only wouldn't she do it, she wouldn't even talk about it. Another couple I interviewed for this book with exactly the same problem handled it quite differently. The man's erections were fine but orgasm was difficult to reach without anal stimulation, something he discovered in masturbation. Although the couple had never engaged in this practice before, both were willing to experiment with it and did. The result was more frequent and easier to reach orgasms for him.

By being open to possibilities and change, Lovers protect what they enjoy and keep the ball rolling.

Suggestions

Ask yourselves these questions:

 Is it possible that your mate has been complaining about something that's a problem for him or her that you haven't understood in that light because it's not a problem for you? Have there been remarks about how late you come home from work, how tired you always are in the evening, the amount of time you spend watching sports or the shopping channels on the tube? Can you understand how such things might be bothering your sweetheart and negatively affecting your relationship and love life? Is there anything you're willing to do about it?

 Who or what do you most blame for the lack in your love life? No matter what your response, can you let go of the complaining long enough to ask what you could do to change the situation? Are you willing to do that several times or for several weeks just to see what difference it makes?

Chapter 10

What's Health Got To Do With It?

> "Although the world is full of suffering, it is also full of the overcoming of it."
>
> —*Helen Keller*

In the last chapter, we looked at how Lovers and other couples deal with everyday obstacles to romance, the kinds of things that every couple runs into on a frequent basis. In this chapter, we turn to a more serious kind of barrier.

Perhaps the major obstacle to a good quality of life and active and satisfying sex is the presence of serious medical problems. Discussions of aging tend to focus heavily on physical well-being. In their important work on "Successful Aging," for example, authors John Rowe and Robert Kahn talk so much about the importance of good health (1998, p. 39) that you're likely to get the idea that unless your health is close to optimal, aging is going to be a horrible experience. We may be left with the impression that anyone who has a disease is a failure at growing old.

Of course no one in their right mind is going to argue for poor health. We all want as much physical vitality as is possible. Unfortunately, not everyone at any age is in great condition and sooner or later we all fall prey to some medical disaster. After all, people do not typically go along in near perfect health and then one day suddenly keel over dead. They usually go through a period, in many cases a very long period, of deteriorating well-being. Are we to assume that if we're not in great physical condition, that if we have this or that serious medical ailment, we cannot enjoy good sex? A lot of people seem to hold this belief. Yet I suggest the benefits of good health and the limitations of poor health have both been exaggerated at least as far as good relationships and good sex are concerned. I also suggest that we need to reexamine the way we talk about old age and physical well-being. The time of life after 45, and especially after 60, is the time of disease and disability. It doesn't matter how many veggies you eat and how much you exercise, the odds are that sooner or later you're going to come down with something disagreeable. The real question becomes how can one preserve the highest possible quality of life even with the ailment and the limits it imposes.

It's a fact that serious physical illness or handicap is one of the main reasons many people give for ending their sex lives. When I have given presentations based on my research, many in the audience automatically assume that Lovers are the lucky ones who enjoy near perfect health and well-being. Many couples whom I see in therapy stopped having an active sex life when they were diagnosed or treated for this or that disease or condition.

What's interesting about this is that the Lovers I interviewed have not let these conditions, illnesses, and treatments get in their way. People who have serious medical conditions and disabilities, and who have received serious and invasive treatments for these conditions, can and do have good sex. The Lovers excel at this and in looking at how they deal with health problems, we get yet another perspective on how they implement their resolve to continue to have good sex.

We have already encountered one example of fulfilling sex despite serious medical problems in the story of Betsy and Wade in Chapter 6. Recall that Wade had a stroke and heart problems and that Betsy suffers from glaucoma, an autoimmune disorder, and vulvadynia. They are both taking a number of powerful medicines. But they are not the only ones who are enjoying sex in the face of serious medical disorders. In the remainder of this chapter, I present several other cases that I hope will help dispel any myths you may hold about sex and serious illness and open your mind to what is possible.

One caveat before we begin. The couples in this chapter were not chosen at random. Each includes more than one serious medical ailment and one or more may sound so dramatic and complex that the reader may wonder if they are a combination of several cases. I assure you the stories are true and are not composites. I chose them because I believe they show how you can maintain good sex despite profound limitations better than cases with less serious or fewer medical complications.

Pearl and Ron

This couple is in their middle 50s and report that their marriage and sex life, always good, have steadily improved over the three decades of their togetherness. They "communicate more straightforwardly and more honestly, and are more vulnerable." Pearl says that "things about Ron that used to annoy me, or even piss me off, I now find quite tolerable and sometimes endearing," and Ron says that he's become "more loving, more present, more considerate." Pouting and withdrawal, in which each had engaged at times, have all but disappeared.

Sex has always been an important part of their relationship. Their communication around sex is excellent. Ron says that they've trained each other about what kinds of things they do and don't like. He also notes that they've been willing to talk about difficulties when they arose, such as his desire to get to her genitals as quickly as possible and her desire that they take more time. Both enjoy erotic videos and magazines and often use them as part of lovemaking. The same is true for smoking marijuana and sharing sexy fantasies.

Pearl doesn't lubricate as much since menopause but they don't consider this a big problem. Desire and frequency have decreased a bit. They now have sex about twice a week. Earlier on, they had a desire discrepancy, with Ron wanting sex more often than Pearl. But his libido has waned some while hers has held steady, so the discrepancy no longer exists.

Ron has always been a quick ejaculator. "My strategy for dealing with this is to make sure that Pearl has already had a bunch of orgasms by oral or manual stimulation before I ever get inside of her. That seems to take care of things, so it doesn't make much difference how long I last when we're having intercourse."

You, the reader, may be wondering what's so special about this case. Except for perhaps the marijuana and the extensive use of erotica, this couple sounds pretty much like other Lovers already discussed. They do have two sexual problems, a desire discrepancy in the early years and quick ejaculation, but there is something else as well—Pearl's medical situation. A few years ago she lost a transplanted kidney, developed hepatitis C, and recently had a heart attack, and two back operations. She has high blood pressure, for which she is on medication, and she is on dialysis. These conditions place at least two types of limitations on their lovemaking. Because her back is not in great shape and because she has a steel rod in her neck, she is limited in the sexual positions she can assume. Sixty-nine, which used to be one of their favorite activities, is no longer possible. Ron mentioned with a laugh that "all these fucking pillows on the bed" used to help Pearl feel comfortable in certain intercourse positions which drove him crazy. Another problem is that Pearl herself would like more intercourse, maybe three times a week, which would be fine with Ron. Unfortunately, she usually doesn't have the energy.

Pearl's illnesses and treatments have taken a toll in another way as well and this kind of situation presents a problem for many couples in which there is a disabled partner. Ron's words about this are instructive: "There have been a number of changes in her body brought about by the illnesses, which made her less of a visual turn-on to me. I went through something interesting with that. One day I was looking at her and realized how misshapen her body had become. I didn't like how she looked. I said to myself, I don't want to see her this way. I don't want to have this reaction. I love her; I'm going to be with her. I have to find a new frame of reference. And I did. I don't know how I did it or what I did, but something inside me changed and now I like the way she looks. I've embraced it in some way and I don't have this yucky feeling, wishing that she was looking like she used to or like Raquel Welch. I'm happy with how she is and I'm proud of that."

This is an excellent example of acceptance, of coming to terms with something in your partner that can't be changed. In this case, it went even further, to actually liking that something. Lovers do this kind of thing all the time.

Although Ron's medical issues may seem trivial when compared to Pearl's, it's worth mentioning that Ron suffers from the arthritic aches and pains so common in midlife. Sometimes he just tries to ignore them but at other times he has found that smoking marijuana before sex is very helpful. This is not an issue for them because, as already mentioned, they both often enjoy smoking dope as a part of sex.

Karen and Paul

Karen is a few years younger than Pearl but with a list of medical problems almost as long; specifically, over 20 years of multiple cancers including breast cancer, and also heart disease, lung problems, neck problems apparently caused by radiation treatment many years ago, and osteoporosis. Yet she and her husband of over 30 years report a wonderful marriage and sex life. It wasn't always like this. Karen says that both she and Paul had a lot of growing to do before they could build the relationship they have now. Regarding herself, she says that when she first met Paul, she was looking much more to him to satisfy all her needs, wants, and desires, which of course put considerable pressure on him and made for a lot of tension in the marriage. She continues: "As I've matured and become better at fulfilling those needs myself without relying on another person, it's taken a lot of burden off my husband and I am able to enjoy him more for who he is versus what he can do for me. As I develop myself and become more aware of who I am and who he is, I've not had the need to fulfill myself through him in the ways I did previously. I am having needs and wants met through that relationship and through him, of course, but it's on a whole different plane, a much healthier plane."

Paul has also made significant changes, the most important one being a shift of priorities. "When we first met," Karen says, "his number one priority was work. This is no longer the case. I moved to the top of his list and that has made for a lot of great changes."

With these alterations, the relationship has gone into high gear and is now something they both treasure and take pride in. As Karen says, "Without question, our marriage is the number one priority for both of us. We make time for each other. I believe there has to be a certain quantity in order for there to be quality. Touching is very important to us and we do it nonstop. We also frequently give compliments and appreciations to each other. There's the 'I love you's, but there is also the 'Gee, you look great in that outfit'. We are there for each other all the time, no question about it. And Paul has been fantastically present and supportive with regard to all my health problems. I marvel at how he has stayed with me despite the issues. There are many men who would not have done that."

Like all Lovers, Paul and Karen adore being together. Most of their social life involves just the two of them—going to talks and shows, taking short vacations (short because they fear being too far removed from the doctors and clinics they are accustomed to), and eating in fine restaurants. The couple has numerous friends and relatives within easy distance, but they limit how much time they devote to them because of their desire to be alone together. The one thing Karen and Paul do not do, however, is engage in athletic activities together because Karen's medical problems don't allow her to do anything athletic except for swimming. This did present a problem at one time because Paul is a golf enthusiast and likes to play as often as possible. Because of her situation, Karen can't play at all; she can't even walk the course. Golf takes a long time, so when he went off to play, they would be separated for half the day on a Saturday or Sunday and they didn't like this. She doesn't begrudge him his interest, and in fact supports it, but what to do about all the time apart? It was Karen who came up with a solution: she often goes with him, taking *The New York Times* to read in the golf cart when he's too busy with the game to attend to her. When he has a few minutes free from the game, they schmooze, joke around, do a little touching, and she reports anything interesting she got from the newspaper.

According to Karen, lovemaking has improved over the years despite the medical reverses.

> To me, there are two parts to sex, the mechanical and the emotional. Because we've had a lot of time to practice, the mechanics have gotten better and better. And because the nonsexual part of our relationship is so much better than when we were first married, sex has become for me personally much more meaningful. I think trust, which took years to build, is the most important variable. Because of the complete trust I feel with him, there is a complete freedom of sexual expression. Because of the trust, I am willing to truly let go when I'm being sexual, and that's exhilarating. I do what I want, say what I want, and let my battered and misshapen body just hang out there as it will. I'm free.

Karen's physical problems have significantly affected the couple's sex life. For example, her feeling of desire, having diminished some as a result of menopause (and because of the drugs she's on, she cannot take estrogen replacement therapy), does not dictate lovemaking frequency. And because she recently suffered a spontaneous bone fracture and was diagnosed as having severe osteoporosis, there had been no sex or over a week, even though she had been feeling desirous.

"I don't know enough about the osteoporosis to know what's allowable and what isn't, what will cause another bone to break and what won't."

Frequency can be a problem for them in another way as well. Sometimes they make love twice a week, but when Karen is having a flare-up of one of her medical problems or she is receiving a particularly obnoxious new treatment, she might not have the inclination or energy, and they might go three or four weeks without sex. But they are always aware of their desire to make love, so as soon as Karen is feeling up to it again, and sometimes even before she's quite up to it, they go for it. There's less intercourse than before because of Karen's discomfort with it: "The oral and manual stimulation have always been important parts of our lovemaking, usually preceding intercourse. Now, because of my problems with intercourse, typically we do the oral and manual without intercourse. And it still feels great."

Something Karen said earlier, about how supportive Paul has been through all of her medical travails, deserves further attention. Pearl said something similar about her husband, as have other Lovers, men as well as women. Whether legally married or not, Lovers take with utmost seriousness the promise, "for better or for worse, in sickness and in health". No matter how painful the issues that arise, they stick with their partners and do all that they can to make the best of the situation. There are a great many other couples for whom this does not happen. From Non-lovers and Lovers speaking about previous relationships I heard story after story about partners who were not supportive, helpful, or even present. Several women gave reports of their partners not being with them in the hospital or even in town when they gave birth. One woman recounted that when she had cancer, her husband (now ex-husband) took her to only one of her medical appointments. He was angry and started screaming at her in the car on the way to the doctor's. He left her at the medical building with her "crying and feeling worthless". Needless to say, he was not there for her surgery either.

Although most of these accounts of being and feeling abandoned feature a man as the perpetrator, it's not only men who act in such ways. Several years ago when I had an operation to remove my colon (a colectomy), my girlfriend disappeared. We had been involved for a number of months and our agreement was that she would be there for me during surgery and recuperation. Soon after the operation, I sensed something was wrong. Paradoxically, it was her oft-repeated statement about how well I was doing that aroused my suspicion. She kept telling me, the surgeon, the nurses, and the visitors how good I looked and how much color I had in my face. It took me several days to figure out what she was up to—trying to deny that I had serious health problems and needed her attention and help. Shortly after I returned home from the hospital, she called to say she was overwhelmed having to care for me, this despite the number of friends and relatives who were pitching in to look after me, as well as a paid nurse. In any case, she said she needed to take a break. I said that would be fine, thinking she would reappear in a few days or a week. It's now several years since that conversation and her break is still going on—I never heard from her again. Apparently, she did not want to be in a romantic or any other type of relationship with someone who had serious, though not life-threatening, medical problems.

Obviously, Lovers don't behave in this way. To them, such behavior is an abomination. To maintain a good sexual connection, especially when you have health problems, you need a partner who is committed to being there with and for you, to offer solace and support, to work with you on finding solutions to problems that come up. These traits, of course, are integral aspects of being a Lover.

Frank and Carla

Frank and Carla met when in their late 40s. Each had been divorced. Carla had been single for almost ten years and dated a lot but was beginning to despair of ever finding a suitable long-term partner. Frank had been dating for two years and he too was starting to wonder if he would ever be in a relationship again. Then they met and the sparks flew.

Ten months after meeting, they bought a house and moved in together. They had what they both described as a close, warm, and lustful relationship and an interesting way of dealing with conflict. If they couldn't resolve an issue on their own in a week or so, they would go to the therapist that Frank had seen when he was getting divorced. Usually, only one or two sessions, each lasting one to three hours, was required.

They made love virtually every single day, a practice that had been going on since they started having sex 11 years before. Experimentation was common. They had sex standing up in the shower, in every room of the house including the hallways, and even several times in the car parked near a lake they enjoyed visiting. Manual stimulation, oral, anal, sex with a vibrator and dildo, sex with dirty talk and sharing fantasies, sex after watching erotic videos or reading erotic stories—you name it, they did it. They had more sex and more varied than most of the other Lovers I interviewed. Everything was terrific and they could hardly believe their good luck. And then Frank was diagnosed with prostate cancer. After spending months researching the treatment options, they decided on surgery. According to their surgeon, this should not affect his erectile abilities. Despite this assurance, Frank did experience erectile failure after surgery. He usually could not get an erection; if he did, he would soon lose it. And this affected him deeply. "I felt bewildered and lost, I didn't know what was happening or why, and I got to feeling very blue, very down. It's like all the good things in my life—my work, my relationship with Carla—all of a sudden they didn't mean a thing. There was no joy left." Carla says it was very hard to be with Frank at that time. "He was alternately depressed and angry," she recalls, "angry at the surgeon, angry at the world, angry at God. At times I found it impossible to be around him." As Frank's dark mood deepened, the distance between the two widened and sex became rare. He even refused to go to see his therapist.

One morning, after several months of despair, Frank found himself reflecting in a calm way about his situation. "It's like I had this wake-up call. I was making myself and Carla miserable. How could I be wasting our lives this way? I had a problem, but hey, that's what I personally, and Carla and I as a couple, were good at, solving problems. We had difficult situations before. Dealing with her son's drug problems was no picnic and neither was dealing with my mother's illness and death. In each case we just sat down over a cup of coffee and discussed the situation and the options. I'd put in my two cents about this and that, she'd give her point of view, and we'd thrash it out and come up with a way to go. That's what was needed now because I was dealing with the most god awful situation I've ever had. I felt like a total piece of garbage and I was letting that feeling get in the way of doing something to fix the problem. I decided to put my sad and angry feelings behind me and work with Carla to get back to our wonderful life."

And that's exactly what he did. Carla was delighted when he opened up and told her he wanted to work toward a solution. They had an appointment with the doctor where they were told that although the operation should not have interfered with his penile functioning, it was impossible to know for certain if any nerves had been cut. Frank was given a gizmo called a RigiScan to take home and hook up to his penis while he slept. It measured the number and rigidity of erections while he slept. The results confirmed Frank's waking experience. Although there were some erections, they were fewer than normal and less rigid. Apparently, some nerve damage had been done.

While all this was going on, Carla and Frank starting having sex again. It had been months since they last made love and the first time was somewhat awkward. "It's amazing," recounts Frank, "that after all that sex we had, every day for years on end, and now it felt like being with a stranger. We really had to get used to each other again." They decided in one of their conversations that since Frank had this erection problem, there would be no attempt to get him hard. That could easily lead to frustration and bad feelings if it didn't work. They would ask for whatever they wanted and do whatever they wanted, and that's it. With oral stimulation, Carla had her first orgasm in more than three months. "It felt so good," she said," "I'd almost forgotten how good it was. To make up for lost time, I asked him to keep his tongue working and I had another, then another, and more and more. I think I had about a dozen. Absolutely delightful. We stopped when I was exhausted and then I started playing with him. I wanted him to feel as good as I did. He got a partial erection and I just kept on going up and down. He had a hard time coming, mainly I think because he was still dealing with his feelings of not having a full erection. But eventually he had a great orgasm. You should have seen it, there was this big, beautiful smile on his face. I hadn't seen that smile in a long time. When I saw it, I knew for sure we were over the worst of our worries."

Frank was not quite done with his anger and depression. In the year that followed he had a few bouts of both. Although this was a big improvement from the previous four months, he was not pleased. He went back to the therapist alone and after six or seven sessions he felt much better.

Rather quickly this couple resumed their old sex life with one exception, no intercourse. Although they enjoyed their activities, they both also missed intercourse. Looking at the options for getting erections, they chose penile injections. At first, Frank had trouble injecting himself. He would often inject in the wrong spot and cause internal bleeding, bruising, and no erection. One day, Carla suggested she try it and it went fine. The injections have worked very well since she started giving them, always leading to an erection more than sufficient for insertion and thrusting.

Carla and Frank soon had another health problem to deal with. About a year after the prostate surgery, Frank's doctor told him that his cholesterol was at an astronomic level and had to be decreased because Frank's family had a history of heart disease. Both his father and an uncle died of heart attacks in their mid 60s. Frank was put on a fiber-rich, low-fat diet, which Carla joined him on, and both started a program of moderate exercise. They bought three pieces of exercise equipment and put them in the spare room in front of a television set. Usually they exercise together but if one is not available, the other watches the news while working out. Here's what Frank says about the new regimen: "Eating the new way and exercising has had unexpected benefits. I've not only brought my cholesterol down, but I also lost 10 pounds and look great—what the kids call buff, I think—and it's helped in sex too. I'm much more active, I have more energy and strength to move around and support my weight and sex feels better. I don't know how anything can be better than what we had, but it really is. The sensations are stronger and the orgasms feel even more intense. I know I sound like a salesman for a gym equipment company, but it's the truth."

This would be a great place to end this report: things were bad for a while but now everything is fine. Unfortunately, that isn't exactly the case. A year before I interviewed them, a routine medical appointment led to the finding that Carla has a leaky valve in her heart. While surgery may be necessary in the future, for now Carla, Frank and their doctors are waiting, watching, and testing. One consequence of this impairment is that Carla has experienced a sharp reduction in her energy level. She now naps almost every afternoon and isn't always up for lovemaking.

Despite this latest medical issue, Carla and Frank continue to think they're fortunate in having one another. Their relationship is as close and loving as ever, and although their desire for sex has decreased some in recent years, especially Carla's, they still make love two to three times a week. Not bad for a couple in their late 60s with multiple medical problems who've been together over 20 years.

Ben and Abby

Ben has been diabetic his whole adult life (42 years now) but until a few years ago was not very limited by the disease. Beginning in his early 50s, a gradual change started taking place in his penis. It took years but he finally ended up absolutely impotent. His diabetes has also caused complications that result in frequent and unpredictable abdominal pains.

According to Ben: "At first my little friend, which for many years had served me so loyally and so well, became unreliable. Sometimes it would stand up, at other times not, regardless of how much stimulation was applied. Failure became the rule and I started relying on penile injections to get hard. Then one day I finally had to face it: I was completely impotent. Neither a partner's nor my own stimulation had much effect on it. Only with the injection would it get hard. I eagerly awaited the introduction of Viagra and then suffered a huge disappointment. After trying the little blue pill in every dose and every time of day and night, it was clear that I, like many other diabetics, did not respond to it. So I went back to the injections."

Ben was not a happy camper. He was alone and wanted a relationship. In his life he had had a number of relationships, and although each had periods of caring, affection, and ecstatic sex, none lasted more than a few years. He wanted something lasting. Although Ben felt more than ready for that better than ever, until-death-do-us-part relationship, he was more than a little concerned about finding it. Who, he wondered, would want a relationship with a 59-year-old guy who was falling apart physically and sexually?

Then along came Abby and after a few dates Ben knew he had found what he was looking for. "We both had committed ourselves to do better than our poor track record in relationships indicated, and I told her up-front about my diabetes, pain, and penis problems. She was understanding and accepting."

Abby and Ben have been together for three years now but it's already clear that this is the best and most mature relationship they have each ever had. Ben continues: "We had some rough times early on—misunderstandings and such—but we dealt with them in ways that made us feel good. We were actually acting the way we thought adults should act instead of following blueprints laid down unconsciously in childhood and in our prior relationships. We talked incessantly and really heard each other. We fought fairly, we brought up and dealt with issues and complaints quickly, we touched constantly and exchanged positive looks and compliments many, many times each day."

How do they keep their sexual relationship good despite Ben's medical problems? In a number of ways. "Because I can feel sick at any time without warning, we do not defer sex. If we're feeling sexual and I'm feeling well, we go for it right then. No putting off sex until Abby eats or until we've run a certain errand or until after we've seen a movie. Since there's no guarantee I'll be feeling well later, we take our pleasure as soon as we can."

As was the case with Karen earlier, Ben's libido does not necessarily dictate his behavior. There are times when he feels desire, but because he also feels yucky, he doesn't initiate sex. There are also times when he is worse than yucky; he has severe pain which kills all desire and any willingness to have sex. Although Ben and Abby typically have sex once or twice a week, Ben has no doubt there would be more if he were pain free more often.

Ben's doctors decided that in order to keep his pain to a minimum, he should wear a Fentanyl (a cousin of morphine) pain patch continuously. Not only do these patches help reduce his pain, but there has been no discernable negative effect on his sexuality.

When Ben and Abby were first together, Ben usually used an injection to get an erection before they had sex.

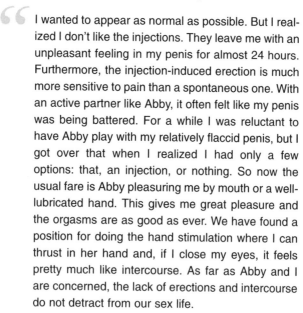

I wanted to appear as normal as possible. But I realized I don't like the injections. They leave me with an unpleasant feeling in my penis for almost 24 hours. Furthermore, the injection-induced erection is much more sensitive to pain than a spontaneous one. With an active partner like Abby, it often felt like my penis was being battered. For a while I was reluctant to have Abby play with my relatively flaccid penis, but I got over that when I realized I had only a few options: that, an injection, or nothing. So now the usual fare is Abby pleasuring me by mouth or a well-lubricated hand. This gives me great pleasure and the orgasms are as good as ever. We have found a position for doing the hand stimulation where I can thrust in her hand and, if I close my eyes, it feels pretty much like intercourse. As far as Abby and I are concerned, the lack of erections and intercourse do not detract from our sex life.

Life with Abby is everything I could ask for. We touch all the time, we have good times no matter what we are doing, we are very open with one another, we talk before, during, and after sex, we joke and laugh, we ask for what we want, and her sighs and moans are music to my ears. Sex is a great comfort and an indescribable delight. Despite my physical limitations, I have everything I want and need.

Here's what Abby has to say:

The quality of my sex life is the best it's ever been. I look forward to each encounter with great anticipation. I cherish our lovemaking because I love giving Ben pleasure and I know he loves pleasuring me. He makes me feel special and like I'm the only one in the world for him. I'm so happy to finally have met a man who loves to touch and kiss as much as I do and who's such a good kisser. Trust me, they're hard to find.

I'm having more fun and more orgasms than I ever did, and the orgasms are unbelievably intense. Before Ben, I didn't know I was capable of having so much pleasure. He is very romantic and creative. He introduced me to vibrator stimulation, so now I'm orgasmic with hand, mouth, and vibrator. We experiment with sex toys and I swear, if we get any more vibrators and dildos, we'll be able to open our own store.

Yet, despite all the experimentation, their sex is very intimate.

> No matter what else we're doing—laughing, sharing a fantasy, playing a game, experimenting with a new toy—it's always making love. There is an incredible bonding that takes place with the looking, the kissing, the caressing, and the holding that goes on before, during, and after. This feeling secures and reinforces the connection and stability of our relationship.

Regarding the limits posed by Ben's medical problems, Abby had this to say:

> Our situation isn't perfect. Ben's health puts some restrictions on us. We can't make love when he has one of those pain attacks and they make me feel terrible. I feel so powerless to do anything for him at those times. To be honest, once in a while I miss the actual act of intercourse, the feel of his whole body on mine and his penis in me. He offered to get a penile implant, but after visiting the surgeon with him to hear what that entailed, I knew it wasn't worth it. Everything else we do in our lovemaking more than compensates for the lack of intercourse. By and large, I'm not troubled by his lack of erections and the absence of intercourse.
>
> One reason for my contentment is that we found a partial solution for the absence of intercourse. I realized that what I missed most of all was having his body cover me and the feeling of all his weight on me. So I suggested that he just lie on me and we've been doing a lot of that. He gets on top—you know,

> missionary position—and we either lie still or dry hump for five or ten minutes. That does a lot for me.
>
> I am concerned about his health and well-being and sometimes I worry about what the future will bring. All in all, however, I love what we have and not a day goes by when I don't thank my lucky stars for giving me such a wonderful romance and sex life. To be honest, I thought that perhaps I had missed my chance and that I might be too old to start again. I'm so happy I was wrong. I am truly blessed and wouldn't trade our relationship for anything in the world.

Certainly Pearl, Karen, Carla, Frank, and Ben, as well as Betsy and Wade, have more than enough justification to stop having sex altogether. They all have serious illnesses and are taking very high-powered drugs, several of which are known to inhibit sexual desire, and they are often exhausted from their conditions and treatments. Yet because these couples want to have sex, and high-quality sex to boot, they deal with their situations and have the great lovemaking they want. They may have had to change how and when they have sex, but all in all it's worked out.

Are these situations and solutions perfect? Not at all. Each of these couples would prefer to have things otherwise. Pearl and Karen would prefer better health and more energy, as would their partners. Carla and Frank would also prefer better health, as well as more energy for Carla, and Frank and Ben would like it better if they sometimes had the option of an erection and intercourse without taking an injection. So no, their lives are not perfect. That's the bad news. The good news is that their relationships and sex are damn good and they are all grateful for that.

Among the Lovers I interviewed, almost every single medical disaster—illness, disability, discomfort, what have you—is represented. Among them: angina, arthritis, back and neck problems of many types, Cogan's syndrome, breast and prostate and many other types of cancer including Hodgkin's disease, diabetes both Type 1 and Type 2, diverticulosis, heart conditions of many descriptions and treatments including medicines and open-heart surgery, lupus, sleep apnea, stroke, thyroid problems, and vulvadynia. There were also specific sexual difficulties, especially erection problems for men and desire and arousal problems for women. Yet all the Lovers dealt with their problems and ended up with satisfying sex lives that they are proud of.

I imagine that some readers, despite having read this far, are still somewhat resistant to the idea, even the possibility, of sex in the face of ill health. In a last attempt to persuade you that what I say is not only possible, but commonplace, I offer a rich example that has nothing to do with my research.

It's the story of Virginia and Keith Laken, which I learned about from their book *Making Love Again* (2002), as I was completing my work. It tells of their several-year struggle to reestablish a good sex life after surgery for Keith's prostate cancer destroyed his ability to have erections without penile injections. Their adventure was long, arduous, and filled with frustrations and failures, more so than any couple I interviewed, but they finally emerged with a satisfying sex life, though quite different from the one they had before the surgery. As Keith put it:

> Next to my recovery from cancer, I've found that reestablishing physical intimacy with Gin has been the greatest gift I've ever received. I love sharing my life with her again—body and soul.

No one would suggest that disability or ill health is a good thing. Yet Pearl, Karen, Frank and Carla, Ben, and others prove that even with disabilities and horrible diseases, good relationships and satisfying sex are still possible. It isn't the physical condition that determines the quality of one's relationship and sex life, it's the attitude, intention, and mind set of the people involved.

This attitude extends to more common and less serious illnesses and conditions as well. In my therapy with couples who don't have much sex, virtually everything in the universe becomes a rationalization for *not* making love. Someone had the flu or a cold or a sore neck or back. Lovers also have flu and colds and sore necks and backs, but with them there are very few reasons for not making love. For several months, Abby had serious back pain, serious enough to warrant two cortisone injections. Did that stop them from having sex? No, because as she puts it:

> It's hard to imagine any good reason for not having sex. Besides, the great sensations of sex help me forget the back pain for a while.

Here's another example of this attitude:

> My back was killing me for several weeks after I injured it in kick-boxing class. My doctor didn't know what to do, neither did the chiropractor, and the drugs they gave me helped only a little. Pete and I tried one intercourse position that felt fine at the time but hurt like hell afterward. But we discovered that rear entry was good, as was missionary with my legs kind of flat. So all in all my back injury affected our sex life only minimally.

One last example:

> I guess most people might think we're strange, but we don't stop making love just because one of us has the cold or flu unless, of course, that person just doesn't feel like it or is vomiting or has diarrhea. Look, we sleep in the same bed, breathe the same air, eat out of the same dishes. If one of us gets sick, there's a good chance the other will too. So what? It's a good excuse to take a day or two off work. Sometimes when one of us is ill, we still have intercourse, sometimes a hand job, sometimes oral. It's whatever we want and it works fine for us.

No one is saying you have to make love when you have the flu or your back hurts or if you have a chronic or acute serious illness; in fact, no one is saying you should have sex at all unless you really want to. But I hope the examples in this chapter gave you some ideas of what's possible for those with limitations who are interested in maintaining a nurturing and loving relationship.

Suggestion

 Ask yourself if you have been using a physical malady or its treatment as a reason for not having a superior sex life. Have you retreated from sex, or more frequent sex, or more satisfying sex, because of this or that ailment? Then ask if that's OK with you or if you'd like better lovemaking. If your response is the latter, what are you willing to do about the situation, what specific steps are you willing to take to make things better? Then visualize yourself taking those steps (start with the easiest ones first); for example, talking with your partner about your desire to rekindle the flame; initiating sex with him or her as soon as possible; accepting his or her next advance instead of rejecting it as usual; or talking with your physician about taking, reducing, or discontinuing a certain medicine. Instead of giving up because of your illness or disability, why not look on the bright side and make the best use of your assets and strengths, just like the examples in this chapter.

Chapter 11

Effective Sex Talk

I suspect that most Americans by now are thoroughly sick and tired of having experts, so-called experts, and pseudo-experts hector them on the need for greater communication with loved ones, colleagues, friends, and others. For several decades now, relationship experts, sexologists, talk show hosts, and anyone else with access to a microphone, pencil, or computer have been telling us about the need to communicate in relationships, work, and sex. It seems everyone is telling us we ought to do more talking. According to my research, this advice is right on target—and not.

The reasons we are tired of hearing the same message over and over are two: first, talking is more difficult than the experts indicate; second, it doesn't always work! We try, we rehearse our speeches in our heads, we gather up our courage and tell our loved ones what we want to get across, and bam, it doesn't make things better. In fact, at least half the time, it makes things worse. A situation that before was bad but tolerable now becomes unbearable. Once having been broached, it's no longer possible for the topic to be squeezed back into the hole whence it came. Now it's right there in the middle of things, staring us in the face, making both of us feel self-conscious, awkward, and often angry as well. And we don't know what to do about this now. Where are the great media gurus when you really need them?

My sympathies are entirely with the reader or listener. We experts have spent too much time exhorting people to talk without providing information about the risks involved (and you can be certain there are risks to bringing up sensitive topics like sex), without giving sufficient information on the kinds of conversations that help and the kinds that hurt, and also what to do once a sensitive topic is out in the open but seems incapable of resolution. I believe the following discussion of talk among Lovers— and among Non-lovers—sheds some light on crucial issues.

Lovers tend to be talkers, generally and sexually. They talk because it's a way of connecting and sharing, because they want to get their partner's perspective, because it's a way to clear the air, and because it's a way of getting one's own needs met. They don't just talk, they do so successfully. Their conversations work, whether the goal is to make contact, convey information, arouse the partner, or get exactly the kind of stimulation they want. I do not want to give the impression that Lovers continually talk. That is not the case. Some talk more than others; this is simply a matter of personal preference. But all of them use words, as well as other means of communication such as touch, to get across what is necessary or beneficial to the relationship and to the two people involved.

The Lovers use words, as they use just about everything else, to enhance the quality of their erotic lives. It's not that other couples don't talk at all, but Lovers seem to do it more frequently than most and certainly in more beneficial ways. This is especially true before, during, and after lovemaking. Since I have given many examples of nonsexual talk earlier in the book, I focus in this chapter on talk that has to do with sex or occurs during sex.

To give you an idea of what is to come, let me say this for now. Lovers' talk tends to emphasize the bright side, generally positive and encouraging, with lots of nice things about the partner and the relationship. This tenor is a reflection, of course, of the type of relationship they have. The talk of Non-lovers is quite different. It is either infrequent and neutral, pretty much fact-oriented ("the fridge needs fixing", "what's on the tube tonight?") or it is generally negative, hostile, and blaming, and leaves one with a bad taste in the mouth. It's no wonder it doesn't lead to good results. As we already discussed, when complaints are voiced among Lovers, and I assure you they are, the words tend to be tempered by some measure of tenderness and humor; there is little blaming and some kind of resolution is generally reached. When complaints are voiced among Non-lovers, there often is hostility, judgment, and sarcasm. The tenor is anything but warm and the talk can go on for long periods because solutions are very hard to come by under these circumstances. You can see right away why some talks have better outcomes than others.

Enough generalities, let's go to the bedroom.

Talking to set the stage for sex

For most couples sex is something special, but often it comes out of the blue. While this may sound hot and spontaneous, it is not necessarily a good thing. A woman client complained:

> We go through long periods—hours, sometimes days—with virtually no contact. No talking, no touching, not much of anything. Then, suddenly, here he is, trying to French kiss me or groping my breasts. It's a shock to my system. There's no way I can respond positively. At that point he seems like a stranger pawing me.

Another woman also uses the word "shock" to describe how she reacted to her mate's behavior:

> He'd spent hours in the den watching football and suddenly—it must have been half-time or something—he rushes in breathlessly and suggests sex. I mean, *Hello*, where does that come from? And what does it have to do with me? No way I can get turned on like that.

Angie, whose relationship with Richard we discussed in Chapter 5, had the same complaint. By contrast, Lovers are making love or romancing in the broadest sense all the time. Recall what was said in earlier chapters about Lovers' relationships. They spend lots of time together having fun, expressing loving and complimentary words, and affectionately touching. This combination isn't a bad definition of foreplay. Lovers are almost continually engaged in love play or foreplay, so the stage is almost always set to take the action further. To Lovers, sex isn't something set apart from the rest of their relationship. It's just another thing they do, another way they connect and express their feelings, another way they have fun together.

One Lover had a difficult time with my questions.

> The way you're talking," he said, "makes sex sound like a thing apart. Here's the marriage, all the many parts of it and over here, all by itself, is sex. I don't see it that way. Sex is just another aspect of our relationship, another way we bring pleasure to each other, another way we connect. Like it's the perfect way to top off a night out at the opera. But it's not something all by itself and it's not something different than what usually goes on.

Put differently, Lovers have what I call an ongoing erotic connection. With their touches and words, they keep themselves aware that sexuality is one of the things they share. A woman expressed it this way:

> Sex is very important to us and it's never far from awareness. It's like we constantly remind ourselves of our wonderful sexual connection. One way we do this is by our discussions of our last sexual encounter. For days afterward, we make mention of what was especially good about it. Another way is that we also talk about what we want and what it will be like the next time. And there's also the touches. My husband has a thing about my butt. Not only does he constantly talk about it in the most exalted ways, which I

love, but he's always touching and squeezing it, which I also love. And I frequently make comments about Roger, my name for his dick. Given all this, you can see why sex is not fully out of our consciousness anytime. We go around in a constant state of low or mid-level arousal. We're never at zero in that regard.

Yet Non-lovers of any age hardly ever talk about sex except perhaps in the most general ways. I recently had a therapy session with a couple in their late 30s, meaning younger than our sample. They have never talked about sex in any detail, not during sex, not outside of sex. The most they ever say is, "That was good." There's very little information conveyed in that remark except that the event was positive. There's no information about which particular activities were terrific and should be repeated, which ones should be expanded on, and nothing to set the stage for the next time. There's also not much arousal value in the statement. This from our supposedly liberated younger generation! Interestingly, I found this pattern of communication—that is, virtually none—in a number of the Non-lover couples I interviewed.

Because Lovers engage in constant foreplay or love play, it's highly unlikely that they will forget about sex for any period of time. It's also unlikely that they'll need a lot of preparation to get ready or involved. They do in fact spend a lot of time making love but that's a choice they make because they so much enjoy being together this way and the feelings generated by it, not because they need to in order to get the man hard or the woman lubricated.

Some Lovers also set the stage in other ways. As one woman put it:

> We set it up so that we make an environment that will likely lead to sex.

Another woman gave details:

> It has a lot to do with our relationship outside of the bedroom. We are very nice to each other and very respectful of one another. We try to do any unfinished business before we have sex. We transition into sex by talking, taking time to put on the music, lighting the candles, or showering together. Or it might be looking at Penthouse magazine, which I find as arousing as he does, reading sexy stories, or smoking marijuana. He does what he knows will make it possible for me to really relax and get into sex. I try to do the same.

Other Lovers also mentioned taking care of unfinished business before making love. But some didn't and the reason is clear: because Lovers spend a lot of time together and because they talk and bring up issues as they occur, there usually isn't any unfinished business or at least not a lot of it.

Here's another example from a woman in her 70s:

> We hold hands when we talk and in the movies, and we touch knees when something is meaningful to both of us. There's a sexual component to this. Very much so when we are dancing. When we dance, maybe to some nice Al Green music, it's so romantic and we have sexual rubbing against each other. And

> we kiss when we dance. I love to do that and so does he. And sometimes when I'm at the sink, he comes over and rubs my bottom. And he often tells me how much he loves my body and how much I turn him on. There's sexual suggestions and meaning in all of this.

Burning incense and candles, and playing romantic or erotic music are also used by a number of Lovers, often accompanied by romantic or sexy words. Flirting is another way some Lovers set the stage. Here's what one man had to say:

> Jenny and I flirt a lot. We make eyes at each other, we make sly hints about our last sexual experience or what's to come next time, there's lots of *double entendres*, lots of sexual jokes, usually not real crass but the more subtle ones.

This from another woman who is in her 50s and makes love with her partner five to six times a week and is orgasmic 100% of the time:

> I think and fantasize about sex more than a lot of women. I think of sex many times every day. I read a lot about sex, whether erotica or self-help or informational books and articles. I like to engage in sexual touch with my partner … constantly. This, in addition to the physical and verbal innuendos is definitely foreplay for me.

Here's how one Lover described the talking she and her partner do before sex:

> We always spend a half hour or so talking before we make love. We talk about all sorts of things, our lives, our children, how much we love each other, what we would like to do next year, on our next vacation, how much we like our bedroom .... It's just a way of connecting and really allowing ourselves to experience the joy we have in our lives.

Talking during lovemaking

Almost all the Lovers agree that it's necessary to talk during sex, if nothing more than to indicate what one wants or that one is getting what one wants. Pearl, a woman with numerous medical problems whose story I discussed in Chapter 6 said this:

> We are expressive both verbally and extra-verbally [moans and grunts]. Sometimes we talk dirty with each other. We both feel free to say and ask for whatever we want.

That phrase, "We feel free to say and ask for whatever we want," was given spontaneously by the vast majority of Lovers and this should not come as a surprise. Because of their trust and comfort, they aren't afraid to express their desires. Because of their intention to have good sex, they have to talk. Here's what a woman married 54 years says:

> We talk during sex. I feel free to ask for whatever I want now. There were years when I was afraid to. So

> was he. But our communication has improved over time as we've become more open with each other. We now have a verbal freedom that we never had before. Now he tells me that he loves my body and that I turn him on. We make a lot of sexual conversation. There's a lot of feedback during sex about what we like and how we feel.

Asking for what one wants is just one kind of sexual communication. Another kind is expressing pleasure in what one is getting. This kind of talk is often called feedback, and it's something Lovers also do a lot of. The importance of feedback is that it's another way of letting your partner know that he or she is making you happy. This in turn tends to make the partner happy because he or she realizes that what they are doing is having the desired effect. On the other hand, if there is an absence of such communication, the giver wonders if they should continue what they're doing, switch to something else, or what. This kind of doubt is not conducive to focusing and staying aroused.

Yet another kind of sexual talk involves C and A—compliments and appreciations—something Lovers do well. They are constantly expressing how much they like each other's bodies and actions, how sexy they find the other, and how much pleasure they are deriving from what is going on. The effect of frequent and numerous sexual C and A is difficult to exaggerate. The whole atmosphere is radiant, both partners feel wonderful and grateful, and arousal is much easier to attain and keep.

What about the often heard complaint that any kind of talk during sex disrupts concentration and arousal? As one of the Non-lovers I interviewed put it, "I don't like talking during sex. It destroys the romantic mood." Lovers do not see it this way. To them, talking is an integral, necessary, and delightful aspect of making love. As I was writing this chapter, I approached a Lover couple I know and had previously interviewed, and asked them about the issue of talking being a distraction during sex. The woman immediately jumped in:

> No way! It's part and parcel of sex, so how can it interfere? That's like saying kissing or breast stimulation is disruptive. How could that be since they're part and parcel of sex?

The man nodded and said only:

> I'm with her. It's like they're saying putting food in your mouth interferes with eating.

Depending on your own situation, you may think that everyone talks about sex and during sex, or that no one does. Both answers are correct. There are people like our Lovers who have made an art of sex talk. Yet there are many other people who rarely or never talk about sex. Sex therapists will tell you that the vast majority of their clients are almost totally silent during sex. They don't say what they want, they don't express pleasure in what they're getting or doing, they don't give C and A. Given that many partners don't even tell their beloved that they look good in their new dress or shirt, it's not surprising they don't say that their partner has beautiful breasts or a lovely penis.

Several people I interviewed had reasonable sex but didn't rate it highly enough to qualify as Lovers. The main reason in most cases was their inability to talk about sex. Here's how one man expressed it:

> I don't know exactly what it is. We have a pretty decent relationship and sex life, but we've never been able to be real open about sex. Even now, after 20 years of marriage, there are many things I'd be too embarrassed to say to her. I think them, but I just can't imagine myself saying them. She must feel the same because she doesn't say much either. I wish I could be more open, I know it would be good for us, but so far it hasn't happened.

It's clear from this quotation that they haven't even talked about their difficulties with talking. He was guessing that "she must feel the same." He had not gotten the information from her. This man is correct. Talking would be good for them but it doesn't look like it's important enough to either of them to take responsibility for resolving the problem. His concluding words, "so far it hasn't happened", are passive and do not suggest that he plans to do anything about it.

A married woman, not a Lover, described her situation like this:

> We've gotten better at expressing our feelings to each other over the years. Maybe that's damning with faint praise because when we started out we hardly said

anything. But there has been progress and we're both happy about it. Sex, however, is another matter. We've not made much headway there. I don't know why, maybe the strict religious upbringing we both suffered through, but it's just about impossible for us to say anything about lovemaking. We can't even initiate verbally. The closest we come is when I put on a negligee and ask him it he'd like to come to bed, or when he comes up and nuzzles my neck. I know he likes my breasts, he likes to look at them and touch them, but he's never once told me how he feels about them. And I've never told him once that I really like his penis, like looking at it—I think it's kind of cute—and like playing with it. There must be kids in eighth grade who are better at this than we are. But there we are and given how long it's taken for us to open up in other areas, I don't think it's going to happen sexually. And that's sad.

Talking after lovemaking

It stands to reason that people who can and do talk about sex before and during lovemaking will often talk afterward as well. And that's what I found with the Lovers. Many recounted verbally expressing their love and contentment as they held each other. Several mentioned saying "thank you" to their partner for the pleasure just received. These conversations were generally brief—often the partners were tired and looking forward to sleep or a nap—but enough was said to convey closeness, caring, and happiness.

Sometimes, however, there were more extended discussions having to do with the details of what had just occurred, what acts were particularly exciting and pleasing, how to make it even better, or what to do next time. This is a good way to reinforce one's preferences to your partner. Whatever the exact nature and duration of these afterplay discussions, they always included praise and C and A. As one woman put it:

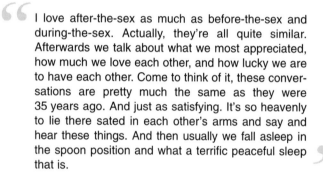

> I love after-the-sex as much as before-the-sex and during-the-sex. Actually, they're all quite similar. Afterwards we talk about what we most appreciated, how much we love each other, and how lucky we are to have each other. Come to think of it, these conversations are pretty much the same as they were 35 years ago. And just as satisfying. It's so heavenly to lie there sated in each other's arms and say and hear these things. And then usually we fall asleep in the spoon position and what a terrific peaceful sleep that is.

Adoration

A lovely trait of many male Lovers is their often-repeated praise of their partner's body, something that is especially important to women as they age. A number of women noted that they did not feel very good about their aging body but that this feeling was mitigated by their partner's praise. One woman said:

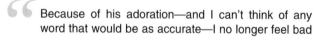

> Because of his adoration—and I can't think of any word that would be as accurate—I no longer feel bad

about myself. He just constantly compliments all my parts. Makes me feel wonderful.

Betsy (Betsy and Wade, Chapter 6), who is in her 80s, described her experience:

If left to my own devices, I'd feel very critical about all the sags and wrinkles. This is not the kind of body they show in movies or TV commercials. But he sees it differently and because of his many compliments and expressions of joy, it's like he lends me his eyes and I no longer feel so self-critical.

Several other women also mentioned seeing themselves through their lover's eyes because of the constant compliments about their physiques.

Another woman made this report:

I felt bad about my butt for many years. It's way too big and jiggly. I was always embarrassed to let a man see me from the rear. But Josh has mainly turned me around on this. He goes on and on about how he loves to look at my behind and touch it. He actually kisses and licks it, says it's so beautiful and erotic. At first I thought he was just flattering me, but over the years I realized he really means it. I have been touched by his words and acts, they changed my attitude. I now feel much better about my butt and, actually, my whole body. If he likes it so much, then it can't be as bad as I had thought.

Many male Lovers mentioned complimenting their partner's bodies and actions, but none bragged about their own efforts. You'd never know from listening to them what an incredibly positive impact their C and A had on their partners.

Using words as well as touches to clear the air and maintain an erotic connection, asking for what you want, giving guidance and feedback, and expressing C and A seem fundamental to having terrific sex. Talking dirty and sharing fantasies are not. Some Lovers do these things, others don't. As long as you can take care of the basics, so that both people are getting what they want and are feeling good about themselves, you're doing fine.

Talking about sex problems

When sex problems occur—whether it be a one-time event when the man doesn't get or keep an erection or when the woman doesn't lubricate as usual or get aroused, or whether it be a chronic situation having to do with desire or functioning—talking is absolutely necessary. Yet the occurrence of problems for many couples makes talking even more difficult because of the embarrassment and shame involved. And when there is no talking, people's worst fantasies take over. The woman whose partner didn't get an erection starts to think he doesn't love her anymore or find her desirable. The man whose partner doesn't lubricate or get aroused as quickly as previously, or have an orgasm, may harbor similar fantasies.

And when chronic conditions occur that may necessitate a whole new approach to sex, the lack of talking often means no more sex at all. In the last chapter I presented the reports of several couples with serious, chronic medical conditions. In all these cases, extensive and continuing discussions were necessary to keep sex alive. Fortunately, all the couples described are Lovers and were able to have these conversations. It wasn't easy— talking about sex often is not easy—but it had to be done and was.

If you're one of those people who have trouble talking during and about sex, you may be able to take heart from the fact that talking is also the aspect of sex that Lovers had the most trouble with. A number noted that they or their partners weren't quite as free and open as they liked. One man said that although he had overcome most of his inhibitions about verbalizing about sex, his partner lagged behind. He'd like her to talk more, but he knows that's not about to happen. A woman Lover reported that although she and her partner of almost 30 years had both improved somewhat in their ability to express their sexual desires over the years, it was still less than ideal. Talking is necessary and helpful, but for many people, even Lovers, it's anything but easy.

The best kind of conversation regarding sex problems is the one I identified as problem-solving in Chapter 9. After expressing whatever feelings need expressing, there should be a specific definition of the problem, what difficulties it is creating, what goal is desired, what resources are available, and which solution to start with.

I think all conceivable solutions should be considered, even ones that seem silly or impractical, just to be sure nothing is left out. Then you can start crossing some off the list because of their disadvantages. If the couple is able to stick with the discussion in a relatively calm way—which, by the way, doesn't have to be completed in one session or one day—more and more options get eliminated and soon one or two emerge as the best choices. This is generally how the Lovers handled their sexual complaints.

Suggestions

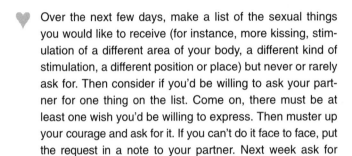 Over the next few days, make a list of the sexual things you would like to receive (for instance, more kissing, stimulation of a different area of your body, a different kind of stimulation, a different position or place) but never or rarely ask for. Then consider if you'd be willing to ask your partner for one thing on the list. Come on, there must be at least one wish you'd be willing to express. Then muster up your courage and ask for it. If you can't do it face to face, put the request in a note to your partner. Next week ask for something else on the list.

The next time you make love, express some version of the following at least once: "That feels [You make me feel] so good", "This is really exciting", "You're driving me crazy", "You're so sexy".

Over the course of several days, make a list of all the things about your partner that you like physically and sexually. If you notice yourself focusing on things you don't like, not to worry. Either skip over them and get to the positive or consider if there's a positive side to any of the negatives. For example, you may find that although you don't like to look at your partner's excess flesh, it feels good to touch. There must be some things about your partner that you like: some body parts, the way they smile, their sexy laugh or manner, the way they caress you, the sounds they make during sex, something. Then, the next time you make love, be sure to express a compliment about at least one of the items (for example, "I love the way you're touching me. It's making me so hot"). In the hours or days afterward, be sure to express an appreciation about something your partner did or said during sex ("I loved the way you touched my breasts the other night. It really turned me on").

Chapter 12

Finally ... Sharing Joy

"So, lively brisk old fellow, don't let age get you down.
White hairs or not, you can still be a lover."
—*Goethe*

"Old Ladies take as much pleasure in love as do
the young ones."
—*Pierre de Bourdeille Brantome*

Our journey is nearing a close, yet there is one more important variable that separates the Lovers from other couples. It's so obvious I'm sure many readers have already asked themselves when I'll get to it. It's simply a great interest in, desire for, and comfort with sexual activity. I know, I know, sometimes our culture seems so driven by sex and so consumed by it that it's easy to get the impression it's all that anyone is interested in. Yet a moment's reflection shows that's not the case. Sure, sex sells and many people take a lively interest in it, but not everyone by any means. Take this fellow, for example:

He was a therapy client to whom I presented some of the findings from this study thinking they would give him hope. I couldn't have been more wrong. He stated authoritatively that the Lovers sounded like they were obsessed with sex and that he considered them to be an extremely unhealthy and dysfunctional group. The last thing he wanted, he said, while pointing a finger at me, is to emulate them or even hear more about them. It is probably not surprising that he was seeing me for his chronic lack of interest in and lack of attention to sex—behaviors that had cost him two marriages.

For this reason, it is imperative that partners are matched sexually as well as in other ways if the relationship is to be mutually satisfying. If sex is not that important to you, if you can take it or leave it, you need a partner who feels similarly. On the other hand, if it is important, you need a partner who feels the same way.

We are constantly advised by well-meaning friends and even therapists that sex isn't everything. No one said it was, but if it isn't working out, it's going to feel like the most important thing in the world and you will become obsessed with it. Many things about sex can be changed and fixed, but mismatched couples are extremely difficult to help. If your partner is not comfortable with sex and isn't all that interested … if your idea of a good vacation is being able to spend hours in bed making love, but your mate feels fifteen minutes is sufficient … if your partner rebuffs a lot of your sexual overtures … do not assume these behaviors will change over the years. Why should they? The chances that the discrepancies will lessen, even with good therapy, are not great. Far, far better to find someone with similar interests and desires.

Likewise, such partners are likely to give up sex altogether if it becomes a hassle, as could happen if one of you develops a health problem that necessitates lovemaking adaptations such as those described in Chapter 10. It's just not worth it to them to spend energy thinking about how to fix the problem. If it's not simple and easy, they prefer to let go of it altogether and move on to other things that are more problem-free.

I have no evidence that Lovers are obsessed with sex, any more than people who love golf, jogging, gardening, or painting and do them frequently are obsessed with those activities. Lovers get a lot out of sex and thoroughly enjoy it. Whether the results they get from sex are what cause them to be so enthusiastic about it, or whether being so enamored of sex has caused the results to be so good, I can't say. But it probably doesn't make any difference. They have been good to sex and sex has been good to them. Dealing with sex as they do generates fabulous experiences, which in turn creates a desire to keep doing it. In psychological jargon, sex is reinforcing to them.

Closeness

A question that immediately arises is why sex is not reinforcing to everyone. There are, after all, couples who have good sex when they have it—but then don't get around to having it again anytime soon. Jesse and his wife (Chapter 2) are like this. He reported that although the sex they have isn't spectacular, it's good enough that often when they do have it they say they should do it more often, and they don't. There are myriad possible reasons for the blocking of reinforcement. From my work with therapy clients in this situation, I suspect in many cases the culprit is a fear of closeness on the part of one or both partners. Sex in a committed relationship is, as all the Lovers and many others acknowledge, a powerful generator of intimacy. But not everyone is comfortable with intimacy. In order to maintain the degree of closeness they can handle, many people have to ration the quantity or quality of sex, otherwise they may produce more intimacy than they think they can tolerate.

The Lovers are different. The crave closeness, pursue it, and rejoice in it. They revel in the delights of connection. Additionally, regardless of where they started out on this dimension they have reached a place where they do not fear closeness. I believe this desire to be intimate comes through in many of the Lovers' quotes I have used in previous chapters. They want to be close, they insist on it, because it means so much to them and provides them with so much delight. This is one of the main reasons, perhaps the main reason, for their success. Lovemaking is just another way to be intimate.

Take the act of talking. Lovers don't talk because some therapist told them it's a good idea. In *The Odyssey*, Homer says that after they were united, Odysseus and Penelope "reveled in each other's stories." One hopes that would be the case given that they had not had seen each other or had any contact for 20 years. There was a lot to talk about. What's fascinating about the Lovers is that they also revel in each other's stories, even though they have probably had contact earlier the same day and what they have to say is not typically about great adventures or tragedies but instead about the mundane vicissitudes of life. They truly want to hear what the partner has to say about their day, their troubles on the commute, their views on current events, their thoughts and feelings about everything. They truly want to learn as much as possible and to keep up to date with this other person. And they also want to share their own experiences and feelings. This is true in and out of the context of sex. What would give her the most pleasure at this moment? Does he like this better than that? How turned on is she at this moment? Is this a good time to switch to a different activity or position? The answers to these questions are very important to Lovers. *Lovers want to know their partners.* They also want the partner to know what gives them the most excitement and pleasure at the moment, what new things they would like to try, what old things they'd like to do again, and how good they feel right now. *Lovers want to be known by their partners.* Knowing and being known are the two basic constituents of intimacy.

Non-lovers do not share these goals. They often do not want to know or be known. A number of Non-lovers told me—Jacob in Chapter 2 is a good illustration—they don't care how their partner's day went, or her commute, or his feelings. And they don't want to express their experiences and feelings to their partner. As far as they're concerned, no news is the best news. Non-lovers and therapy clients often respond angrily when I ask why they don't talk during sex: "Because it gets in the way, it's distracting!" One wonders exactly what they are being distracted from. They don't see, as Lovers certainly do, that talking is another way of being close. Even if it's just to say "do it faster" or "I want to get on top", it can be bonding and a way of being known. Or perhaps Non-lovers do understand this, maybe too well. They don't want to bond any more than they already have and they don't want more intimacy. Perhaps what they're being distracted from is their own fantasies. They want to be somewhere out there, not here in the moment with their partner—that is too dangerous a proposition.

Another area where the Lovers express their desire for and lack of fear of closeness is sleeping. The great majority of the Lovers sleep together in the same bed night after night after night. One man in his 60s mentioned a hurriedly arranged trip that came up that, because of the short notice, his wife could not accompany him on.

> The prospect of being alone in the hotel in Moscow seemed very strange to me. It would be the first time in 40 years that we hadn't slept together. Even when I was in the hospital for surgery, she was there all night and joined me in my little bed. The nurses didn't like it but, to tell you the truth, I didn't give a damn. Her being with me every moment and sleeping with me were the most healing things that happened while I was there.

Not all the Lovers sleep together—a few reported they didn't because of their medical situations and a couple mentioned snoring or restlessness on the partner's part as the reason—and even those who do sleep together do not necessarily do it every single night. For example, although Karen and her husband typically sleep together (Chapter 2), there are occasions when they sleep separately because she is in pain and her body is extremely sensitive to touch.

Lovers sleep together far more than Non-lovers and they had nice things to say about the practice. They talked about how much they appreciated the closeness, how much they liked reaching over and touching their partner, their joy in sometimes finding themselves tangled up together as they slept. They rejoiced in waking up so physically close. By and large, Non-lovers who slept together did not talk this way and, whether they slept together or not, had lots of complaints. They complained about snoring, restlessness, different temperature preferences. All these things, they asserted, irritated them and prevented a good night's sleep. A number of them complained that their partners came to bed late and in the process woke them up. As a result of these complaints, many Non-lovers, and therapy clients as well, decided to sleep apart.

As far as I can tell, as many Lovers as other couples snore, move a lot when asleep, have different temperature preferences, and go to bed at different times. Yet as usual, the Lovers find ways to work with these issues in order to have the closeness they desire.

One group rejoices in and embraces connection, the other fears and runs from it. And this explains a good deal of the difference between Lovers and other couples.

The rewards of sex

As I thought about what Lovers do and what they get out of sex, one phrase kept coming into my mind—sharing joy. This seems to capture better than any other term I've heard about what is going on for the Lovers. They love sex, they love the intimacy that is both a reflection of and cause for their lovemaking, but what's really special about it for them is sharing the physical and emotional joy with their partners. There is a total absence of one-sided sex here. Each partner wants to please the other, not to the exclusion of pleasing themselves, but just because they see sex as a reciprocal activity for two people and because they desire to take good care of each other.

Because of these attitudes and also because Lovers respect their partners, there is a total absence of what I'll call coercive sex. By this term I do not mean rape in the usual sense: there is no use or threat of physical violence. Rather, it's relentless verbal and psychological pressure employed to get sex when the partner is not interested. I've heard of this kind of sex from many distressed couples in therapy with me and it also came up from several of the Non-lovers I interviewed. Here is an example from a woman in her early 60s:

> We don't have a great relationship and we rarely have sex anymore. I mean, I can't even have a conversation with him, why would I want to open my body to him and have sex? I suppose it's hard for him. After all, men have needs, as they all say, even if he's over 60. But I hate what he does. He talks about it nonstop, how deprived he feels, how I'm not fulfilling my wifely duties, how withholding I am, how physically uncomfortable he is—which is weird; I thought blue balls only happened to young guys—and how he feels cheated in the marriage. All he wants is a little loving, why can't I just give him a few minutes? And all the time he's wearing this hang-dog expression which I know is designed to make me feel guilty, and it works to some extent. You have to understand that this stuff goes on all the time: in the bedroom, in the kitchen, in the car, at restaurants, even at the movies. Finally, I give in because I can't take the pressure and guilt anymore. I know that after I give him sex, he'll lay off for at least a few weeks before he starts the same routine again. I give in to gain a few weeks of peace for myself. You know what's really weird? The sex is terrible. I put lubricant in me, lay there, and let him have me. I don't say anything, don't touch him, don't move, don't do anything. I keep my eyes closed and imagine I'm somewhere else doing something pleasant. The whole thing takes only a minute or two. How could he imagine this is a positive experience? Doesn't he realize I'm not really there, that all he's doing is masturbating in me? I just don't understand that.

I passed this last quote by Midge, a woman I had previously interviewed. Now in her late 50s, she has a fabulous romance going with her lover of nine years. I was surprised by her response. She commented:

> " I did almost exactly the same thing with my husband for 20 years. Our marriage was horrid, it was all I could do to get him to give me two or three minutes to talk about the children or house repairs, and our sex was pretty much like what you read to me. I didn't like or respect him enough to want to have sex with him. Making love was so irrelevant to our situation I couldn't even imagine it. But I could only take so much of his criticizing, yelling, begging, and threatening. After a while I'd let him have sex with me just to shut him up. I got absolutely nothing from it except for the deepening of my hatred for him. "

So at least one current Lover lived with coercive sex for many years before moving on to better things. This finding made me wish I had included in my interview schedule an item about coercive sex and gave me reason to believe that this phenomenon is probably more widespread than we think.

Lovers have far healthier and more effective means of dealing with the situation where one partner wants sex and the other doesn't. Emma illustrates one option. Scheduling sex for later or the next day, something many Lovers do, is another.

To Lovers, giving pleasure is as important as receiving it. Each wants nothing more than to pleasure and satisfy their partner. They are not usually looking for a quick release or immediate relief. They are reaching for joy.

Sex is reciprocal in another way as well for Lovers. They seek both the physical and emotional benefits. The men talk about the emotional and relational rewards as well as the physical, and the women talk about the physical rewards as much as the emotional and relational. And they do what they do in a light-hearted, cheerful way. Lovers are not serious or somber about sex. Their attitude is playful. In the interviews with the Lovers there was a lot of laughter. Many had stories to tell of past or recent events that others might take as disasters—being walked in on by children or visiting relatives; an expensive coffee table that broke under the combined weight of the couple; having to explain to a child how his bed, perfectly fine two hours ago, came to be broken; having intercourse in a public place and suddenly realizing there was an appreciative audience; and a woman giving her partner oral sex in a Nordstrom dressing room and suddenly hearing the sales clerk knock on the door and ask if everything was OK—all accompanied by a good laugh. On the other hand, Non-lovers were much more somber and serious about the whole thing. And with clients coming for sex therapy, the atmosphere is grave indeed. No joy at all.

Lovers understand what Sherry Suib Cohen discovered in her own fabulous marriage: "True sexual intimacy is a fine art requiring many cultivated skills, the most crucial being the ability to relax and have fun together"(p. 119). Many others have yet to figure this out.

Because of this lighthearted attitude, there is very little of the performance orientation or anxiety among Lovers. They know or have learned that good sex has nothing to do with performance. They know that good sex has to do with expressing feelings and sharing pleasure and delight. A woman in her 70s married for over 50 years to a man now in his 80s says it like this:

> There is a desire on both our parts to pleasure each other. I did not want a marriage like my parents had; my mother was frigid and my father ran around. I swore to myself that I'd have a marriage that was good in all respects. And that it's been. Our sex is marvelous and so is he. He wants to satisfy me and we take our time. I love the good feeling of being loved and holding one another, touching and kissing, the good feeling of intimacy, pleasure. Afterward I feel relieved and loved. The sexual urge has been addressed. I'm very relaxed, content, and upbeat.

Here are some other examples of what Lovers get from sex: This is from a woman in her 50s whose first marriage was sexually "unfree and horrible". Of sex in her current relationship, she says:

> The physical part is fantastic, it feels terrific and better than when I was 40. It is a part of intimacy, it's an intimacy builder, it's an extension of the trust and the history.

Note that she and the woman quoted before her mention both the sensations and feelings of sex, the physical part, and also the emotional side. This is typical of Lovers' responses.

Here is Karen (Chapter 2):

> There is the physical satisfaction and the physical release. That is certainly one of the benefits. There is

the need for touch that gets satisfied. Early on in the relationship these were the main outcomes and that was fine and satisfying. As we spent more and more time with each other, our relationship has become deeper and richer. In addition there is an emotional need that is being met—which is a feeling of connection, of trust, of acceptance, of not feeling alone. Feeling cared for. Feeling loved. Feeling valued. This is what has added to the richness.

Another woman Lover:

The obvious is the physical release, which is essential. There's this warm togetherness that you have with the other person. A successful lovemaking session enhances the relationship. We are more touchy-feely afterwards and even going into the next day. There's a strong emotional satisfaction that I get from it, more than just the physical.

From a man in his early 60s:

I enjoy giving pleasure and I enjoy receiving pleasure. The orgasmic explosions from my wife are music to my ears and my own eventual explosion is a wonderful, euphoric feeling. It's the highest level of communication that two people can have. We are pretty well bonded and the sex is a reflection of that.

Another man:

It is enormously gratifying to me to give her pleasure. And the converse is true. I derive enormous personal sensory pleasure which is independent from the pleasure I get giving her pleasure. There is emotional closeness and bonding.

This next man adds something different:

You get rid of the urge that's got your mind so focused you can't think of anything else. That's for sure. Release of libidinous urges. Reaffirmation of the bonding of two individuals. It makes me confident that she loves me. I think it does for her too. I guess, I never thought of this before, it is also a reaffirmation that I'm not ready for the grave yet. I've always said that if I lost my ability to enjoy and do sex, I don't know if I'd have anything left to live for. I'm not there yet.

Here's how a woman whose joy in sex is anything but ambivalent describes her experience:

I love everything about sex. I love kissing, I love oral sex, I love intercourse, I love my breasts being stimulated, I love talking, I love looking at each other. I blow all my circuits and get to relax. I clear out all the cobwebs. The physical intensity is very pleasurable. The intimacy is very grounding. If for some reason we haven't made love for a period of time—like if one of us has been sick—we get a little nuts. We get edgy and curt, irritated, it's not a good thing. Lovemaking is a soothing part of the marriage. The connection is very important to us. It's a kind of emotional bonding that occurs that deepens our closeness.

This woman mentions the freedom that menopause has brought her among other things:

> That our bodies are capable of so much pleasure and that there's so much fun. And that it's pure fun and there's no procreation or other reasons. When I was younger and still fertile, we were focused on having children or on preventing having children. Both were a pain. Now that's not an issue. There are no reasons now for having sex other than having pleasure and fun. It's been very liberating being free from that cycle of birth and birth control.
>
> Emotionally I feel a bonding and connection with my lover that is absolutely the most wonderful feeling. The incredible feeling of closeness that makes being in a relationship so special. Sharing the intimacy where there are no boundaries.

Another woman interview shared this:

> I like sex. I like to kiss. I like to hug. I love to give head. I love to be touched. I always liked to do it. As long as I don't have to do butt things and use those green dildos. And of course I like the intimacy, it feels so close and connected.

I'll give the last word here to a man who has a lot to say about what he gets from sex:

> Good sex with my sweetheart is everything good. All my senses are involved. I get to look at her and watch her reactions. I get to hear her and I delight in her little sounds and noises. I get to touch her all over, which I adore. I love being so involved in her flesh, sometimes I get confused between her flesh and mine and it merges and becomes one universal flesh for me to play with and enjoy. I don't have the words

to describe how exhilarating it is for me when she comes. Her body just doubles up and she yells or moans. I feel honored to be part of this.

I'm not forgetting my physical pleasure, which is immense. All the sensations, the tingles, and the warmth, the building tension, and then the great explosion, which releases it all. Sometimes it feels like all my insides are gushing out. And then the sweet peace of lying together and holding each other. The whole thing is very bonding. No matter how close I felt to her before sex, I feel even closer afterwards, and that feeling lingers for hours and days. I think this is what heaven is like.

While the joy and delight of sex is manifest in the Lover's words, it isn't the same with Non-lovers. Sure, many said they enjoyed sex, it felt good, but the richness, enthusiasm, and delight were missing. The expressions of pleasure were bland and cold. As one man put it, "It feels good. It's a great tension reliever." That was it. Not exactly enough to make one want to drop everything and run into bed.

Although I said earlier that Lovers are not obsessed with lovemaking, most of them have come to count on it. If they don't have it for longer than is typically the case for them, they notice. They use these terms to explain how they feel: "irritable", cranky", "edgy", "not quite whole", "distant from my partner". The cure for these feelings, of course, is to have sex as soon as possible. Then, they report, the good feelings return. The negative feelings attendant upon not having sex is a powerful incentive to have it.

When sexual satisfaction is less than desired the issue is confronted head on. An example is a man in his 70s who says that about ten years ago he and his wife went through a period of several weeks where lovemaking was just not up to snuff. At first he thought he might be imagining it, but when he asked his partner, she said she had noticed it as well. They had several discussions about what might be responsible and discovered they were both somewhat distracted. He was in charge of a huge project at work, the most important he'd ever been entrusted with, and she had been made an offer, very hard to turn down, just before she had planned to retire. Both found it difficult to let go of their work concerns. Once this was out on the table, they adopted a solution. Before having sex, they would check in with each other about what they called their "distraction rating". If it was above 4 on a 10-point scale, they would engage in massage or meditation to try to get more focused. This usually helped. When it didn't, they often decided to put sex off for a few hours or until the next day. It is easy to understand how this kind of ability to spot a problem, talk about it with ease, and come up with a solution are powerful tools that keep the quality of lovemaking at a very high level.

Comfortable too

As I hope is clear from the preceding excerpts, the Lovers delight in the many aspects of sex and get a great deal of pleasure from them. Added to this is their relative comfort with sex. I use the qualification "relative" because I doubt that in this largely sex-negative culture anyone is totally at ease with sex, but Lovers seem mainly comfortable with it and certainly more so than those who aren't Lovers. They are easy with the looking; the touching, licking, sucking, biting, and stroking; the odors and sounds; the body parts and fluids; and the various acts. The only physical thing that was a definite turn-off to some women was anal sex. And, as already noted, Lovers are also comfortable with the closeness associated with lovemaking.

A number of the Lovers made it clear that they were not always this easy with sex. Some had to wait until they were in stable and safe relationships, others had to struggle despite relatively high-quality relationships. For most, feeling at ease with sex was a place they reached, not a place they started from. Recall Midge's report; she went from coercive sex in her abysmal marriage to ecstatic sex in a relationship she started at midlife. The interviews made it abundantly clear that being in a trusting and respectful relationship makes a huge contribution to the development of sexual comfort. Lovers know they aren't going to be judged or criticized for their sexual desires, fantasies, and activities. They can be free to express themselves because their partner is not going to punish them for doing so. This is no small thing. It's much more difficult to develop sexual ease when there is a fear that one's words and acts may be judged.

In answer to my question, "What do you like least about sex?" I got a variety of responses from those whose sex lives are not satisfactory: not enough sex, too much sex, not enough foreplay, a lack of playfulness, a lack of creativity, touching that was too rough, touching that wasn't firm enough, needing more time and foreplay than the other person wanted to give, one partner being too timid and on and on. From the Lovers, there was nary anything they disliked. Two of them mentioned the wet spot in the bed, several of the women mentioned anal intercourse, and that was about it. These people really do enjoy and are comfortable with almost all the aspects of sex. It's easy and fun for them, so it's not hard to imagine why they want more of it.

This is not to say, I hasten to add, that every single individual and every single couple is comfortable with everything. Lovers vary in considerably in their sexual routines. Some are pretty intercourse focused, others less so. Some always engage in oral sex, others rarely. Some use sex toys, others do not. Some share fantasies, some don't. Some talk dirty, others do not. Some set the stage with wine, candles, incense, or a bath, others do not. It's not the acts they engage in that sets Lovers apart from other couples. It's how they do what they do and their attitudes toward one another in and out of the bedroom that make the difference. Everyone can be a Lover.

Bibliography

AARP, AARP/Modern Maturity Sexuality Study, 1999

Aldwin, C.M. & Gilmer, D.F., 1999, Immunity, disease processes, and optimal aging. In J.C. Cavanaugh & S.K. Whitbourne, *Gerontology: An Interdisciplinary Perspective*. Oxford University Press.

Apter, Teri, 1995, *Secret Paths: Women in the New Midlife*, Norton.

Baldacci, D., 2001, *Last Man Standing*, Warner Books.

Barbach, Lonnie, 2000, *The Pause*, Revised, Plume.

Barbach, L. & Geisinger, D., 1993, *Going the Distance*, Plume.

Barry, Dave, 1999, *Big Trouble*, Berkley Publishing Group.

Benson, Raymond, 2001, *Never Dream of Dying*, Putnam, New York.

Bland, John H., 1997, *Live Long, Die Fast*, Fairview Press.

Brecher, Edward M., 1984, *Love, Sex, and Aging*, Little Brown.

Bretschneider, J.G. & McCoy, N.L., 1988, Sexual interest and behavior in healthy 80- to 102-year olds, Archives of Centers For Disease Control, MMWR, Internet text edition, mmwrq@cdc,gov, August 11, 2000.

Call et al cited in Hillman 2000.

Cohen, S.S., 1994, *Secrets of a Very Good Marriage*, Penguin.

Cowan, P. A. and C. P. Cowan, 2002, Strengthening Couples to Improve Children's Well-Being: What We Know Now, Poverty Research News 6(3): 18-21.

Cussler, C., 1996, *Shock Wave*, Simon and Schuster.

Daniluk, J., 1998, *Women's Sexuality Across the Life Span*, Guilford.

Duenwald, Mary, 2002a, A conversation with Michael J. Fox, *NY Times*, May 14, D6.

Duenwald, Mary, 2002b, Parkinson's "clusters" getting a closer look, *NY Times*, May 14, D6.

Dychtwald, K., 1999, *Age Power*, Tarcher.

Doherty, William J., 1999, *The Intentional Family: Simple Rituals to Strengthen Family Ties*, Perennial Currents.

Flynn, V,.(2001, *Separation of Power*, Pocket Books.

Follett, Ken, 2000, *Code to Zero*, Dutton.

Foster, R. & Hicks, G., 1999, *How We Choose To Be Happy*, Putnam, New York.

Gagliese, L. & Melzack, R., 1997, The assessment of pain in the elderly. In Mostofsky, D.I. & Lomranz, J. (eds), *Handbook of Pain and Aging*, Plenum Press, pp. 69–96.

Goldberg, K., 1993, *How Men Can Live As Long As Women*, The Summit Group.

Gottman, J.M., 1999, *The Seven Principles For Making Marriage Work*, Crown, London.

Hargrave, T.D., 2000, *The Essential Humility of Marriage*, Zeig, Tucker, & Theisen, Phoenix.

Hillman, J.L., 2000, *Clinical Perspectives on Elderly Sexuality*, Kluwer Academic Publishers.

Hite, Shere, 1976, 1989, The Hite Report: A Nationwide Study of Female Sexuality, revised edition, Dell Publishing Company.

Hunter, S., 2001, *Pale Horse Coming*, Simon & Schuster, New York.

Janus, S.S. & Janus, C.L., 1993, *The Janus Report on Sexual Behavior*, Wiley, New York.

Laken, Virginia & Keith, 2002, *Making Love Again*, Ant Hill Press.

Leiblum, S.R & Segraves, R.T., 2000, Sex therapy with aging adults. In S.R. Leiblum & R.C. Rosen, *Principles and Practice of Sex Therapy*, Guilford, pp. 423–448.

McCarthy, B.W., 1997, Strategies and techniques for revitalizing a nonsexual marriage, *J Sex & Marital Therapy*, 23, 231–240.

McKinlay, J.B. & Feldman, H.A., 1994, Age-related variation in sexual activity and interest in normal men: results from the Massachusetts male aging study. In Rossi, A.S. (ed.), Sexuality Across the Life Course, Chicago: University of Chicago Press, pp. 261–286.

Masters, W.H. & Johnson, V., 1994, *Human Sexual Response*, Little Brown.

Michael, Robert T. *et al,* 1994, *Sex in America*. Little Brown.

Monga, T.R. *et al,* 1999, Coital positions and sexual functioning as patients with chronic pain, *Sexuality and Disability*, 17, 287–298.

Monga, T.R. & Kerrigan, A.J., 1997, Cerebrovascular accidents. In Sipski. M.L. & Alexander, C.J. (eds), *Sexual Function in People With Disability and Chronic Illness*, Aspen, pp. 189–220.

Newsweek, Grannies of the Games, Aug. 14, 2000, pp. 40–42.

O'Reilly, Bill, 2000, *The O'Reilly Factor*, Broadway Books.

Parker, R.B., 2002, *Widow's Walk*, Putnam.

Prager, K.J., 1995, *The Psychology of Intimacy*, Guilford.

Quadagno, J., 1999, *Aging and the Life Course*, New York: McGraw-Hill.

Reeves, T.C., 1991, *A Question of Character: A life of John F. Kennedy*, Free Press, New York.

Rivers, J., 1999, *Don't Count the Candles*, HarperTorch.

Roberts, C. & S., 2000, *From this Day Forward*, William Morrow.

Rowe, J.W. & Kahn, R.L., 1998, *Successful Aging*, Pantheon.

Rubin, L.B., 1990, *Erotic Wars*, Farrar, Straus & Giroux, New York.

Schiavi, Raul C., 1999, *Aging and Male Sexuality*, Cambridge University Press, Cambridge, England.

Schover, L.R., 2000, Sexual problems in chronic illness. In Leiblum, S. & Rosen, R. (eds), *Principles and Practice of Sex Therapy*, Guilford, pp. 398–422.

Smeltzer, S.C. & Kelley, C.L., 1997, *Multiple Sclerosis*. In Sipski, M.L. & Alexander, C.J. (eds), *Sexual Function in People With Disability and Chronic Illness*, Aspen, pp. 177–188.

Starr, B.D. & Weiner, M.B., 1981, *The Starr-Weiner Report on Sexual and Sexuality in the Mature Years*, McGraw-Hill, New York.

Vaillant, G.E., 2002, *Aging Well*, Little, Brown.

Walsh, P.C., 2001, *Dr. Patrick Walsh's Guide to Surviving Prostate Cancer*, Warner Books.

Whitaker, B., 2002, In Hollywood, no one gets a casting call for this role, *NY Times*, Mar. 11, Section E, p. 8.

Wile, D. B., 1999, Collaborative couple therapy. In Donovan, J (Ed.) *Short-term couple therapy*, Guilford, New York, pp. 201–225.

Zilbergeld, B., 1999, *The New Male Sexuality,* revised edition, Bantam Books, New York.

Index

USA & Canada orders to:
Crown House Publishing
P.O. Box 2223, Williston, VT 05495-2223, USA
Tel: 877-925-1213, Fax: 802-864-7626
E-mail: info@CHPUS.com
www.CHPUS.com

UK & Rest of World orders to:
The Anglo American Book Company Ltd.
Crown Buildings, Bancyfelin, Carmarthen, Wales SA33 5ND
Tel: +44 (0)1267 211880/211886, Fax: +44 (0)1267 211882
E-mail: books@anglo-american.co.uk
www.anglo-american.co.uk

Australasia orders to:
Footprint Books Pty Ltd.
Unit 4/92A Mona Vale Road, Mona Vale NSW 2103, Australia
Tel: +61 (0) 2 9997 3973, Fax: +61 (0) 2 9997 3185
E-mail: info@footprint.com.au
www.footprint.com.au

Singapore orders to:
Publishers Marketing Services Pte Ltd.
10-C Jalan Ampas #07-01
Ho Seng Lee Flatted Warehouse, Singapore 329513
Tel: +65 6256 5166, Fax: +65 6253 0008
E-mail: info@pms.com.sg
www.pms.com.sg

Malaysia orders to:
Publishers Marketing Services Pte Ltd
Unit 509, Block E, Phileo Damansara 1, Jalan 16/11
46350 Petaling Jaya, Selangor, Malaysia
Tel : 03 7955 3588, Fax : 03 7955 3017
E-mail: pmsmal@po.jaring.my
www.pms.com.sg

South Africa orders to:
Everybody's Books
PO Box 201321, Durban North, 4016, RSA
Tel: +27 (0) 31 569 2229, Fax: +27 (0) 31 569 2234
E-mail: warren@ebbooks.co.za